Updated

Short Term Missions
Long Term Impact

John Peter Overholt

What others are saying about this book...

"Short Term Missions: Long Term Impact is a fantastic resource for everyone desirous of being a blessing to other nations. John Overholt packages vitally insightful truth in a style that is caring and easy to grasp. John's wealth of experience delivered in story and succinct points helps each of us to be more understanding and effective in global ministry. I'm very grateful to have this resource now and only wish I had it twenty years ago!

Dr. Theodore (Ted) Vail
Associate Director of Foursquare Missions International

In John Overholt's book Short Term Missions: Long Term Impact, you will be inspired both by his personal life story and his teachings. These are not merely theories learned in a classroom: They were learned in the muck and the mire of life experience in the real world. These are not untested, new or fresh revelations from someone who has only begun their journey, but they are the time tested truths learned from someone who has been living out these principles for many years.

When I first met Pastor John and Debbie, he shared his heart for missions and his hunger to see people experience more of the reality of God in their lives, and my heart was immediately knit together with his. I found a kindred spirit in this man of God. As I began preparing my own church family in Canada to become involved in missions, I knew the first place I wanted to go was to Costa Rica. This summer, our church family is getting ready to take our fourth team there to be a part of the miraculous works that the Lord is doing through this couple.

As you open the pages of this book, you will be challenged to look at short term missions in a new and a fresh way. Some people today argue that it is better to just send money to indigenous missionaries who are doing work in their native countries, but I believe that it is vitally important that Canadian and American churches be personally involved in short term missions with feet on the ground. The benefits and blessings to the individual believers, the sending church, and the mission field is indispensable.

My prayer is that the Lord would use this book to stir up your heart today. May you be forever wrecked for ordinary living, and commit to get involved in short term missions at least once in your life. Get rid of your "yeah, but's..." and GO!

Chris Jordan
Lead Pastor of Beausejour Community Church
Author of Supernatural: Contending for Signs and Wonders Today

Forward

Life is lived between two tension points. Almost anything can be put on a continuum to illustrate this tension between what may appear to be contradictory: a paradox if you please. Often, things that appear to be in opposition are merely the other side of the coin. Both have truth and both must be considered when looking at a challenge. I have discovered that most of the time, it is not "either/or" but "both/and. If you can't see both sides of an issue, you are probably too close to one position or another. If you consider only one, you will miss the richness of considering the other side which produces a fuller understanding.

In his book, *Short Term Missions: Long Term Impact*, my good friend John Overholt enters the danger of looking at the two sides of missions. He and I have talked many hours in his Toyota van about the tension and value of people coming from one part of the world to experience missions for a short period of time and the need of having "boots on the ground": those dedicated people who leave the familiar to live in a country and culture and among people who are different and yet the same.

In the 21st Century, the world belongs to the practitioner and not the theoretician. John and Debbie live what they believe. You will enjoy John's subtle humor and fresh approach to the tension that doing missions in the 21st Century requires both long term missionaries that know the lay of the land and can orchestrate successful short term missionaries who come to experience what reaching a different culture looks like and in the process they develop a life-long heart for missions….a win/win.

Some practice but can't teach. This is not true of John. In the pages following, you will enjoy John's practical wisdom and insights on both sides of the missions' coin: short and long and how they can and need to work together.

This is a must read for leaders and people with a heart for missions. Sit back…think…enjoy…you will not be disappointed.

Tom Gardner
Senior Pastor, Sunshine Hills Church in Delta, BC

Introduction

I am not a stranger to missions. After being involved in over eighty short term mission trips and serving, with my wife Debbie, for over eight years as Canadian Foursquare missionaries in Central America, I have learned a few things along the way. Born in Norway, I am pretty sure that in the core of my being, I have some Viking DNA flowing through my veins that puts a longing in my heart to look beyond my borders in search of new lands to explore.

I see great value in Short Term Mission trips and am highly respectful of those who have sacrificed time and resources to reach beyond their borders to minister where culture and language are foreign. Mission groups can be a great encouragement and help when pointed in the right direction.

Over the years, I have heard and read about criticisms that have been addressed towards the validity of sending short term mission teams. Would it not be better to simply send money? Are not the benefits more for the people who are going than for those who are receiving teams? Are we not in danger of creating dependency with our giving or causing unintended harm by our kindness? Are we really making an impact? Is there really a need for full time missionaries anymore? Some of these questions have been addressed in various books that I will refer to later in this book. Although these books take an honest and candid look at some of the obstacles facing the short term mission's movement, I feel they lean heavily towards emphasizing the problems but address lightly the solutions necessary to promote a healthy short term missions program that will produce long term results.

I have discovered that the success of a mission team depends upon several key ingredients that need to be incorporated into the philosophy and strategy of a church's mission program. There is great potential for long term results. If you have a heart for missions, this book will provide valuable insights on how you can begin to develop strategies that will enable short term mission trips to build upon in each other and establish long term relationships with church members and leaders who you are partnering with on the mission field.

I begin by looking at my missionary journey from Canada to Mexico and then Central America and some of the innocent mistakes that I have made along the way. For me Missions was something I had to experience. I did not get it by watching a TV program or listening to a missionary presentation. I had to step out and do it. Only then was I able to understand what Jesus said to His disciples, John 4:32 *"I have food you know nothing about."* To me, my first mission's trip was like being smitten with the mission bug. I got in touch with the very DNA of what we are called to. After twenty seven years as a short term and long term missionary, I began to sense the nudging of the Lord to write this book and to begin to promote the call to short term missions with a long term impact.

My prayer is that this book will challenge and encourage you to rethink th e way you do missions.

Contents

Chapter 1

<u>The Call</u>

"The mission of the church is missions" — Oswald J. Smith

Youth with a Mission

I had never seen poverty up close until I walked into, what our leader called, "the dump" in Juarez, Mexico. When we arrived, I realized that we were in a community similar to any in Canada, except for the fact that there was no electricity, or water lines or street signs; just these little shacks made up of whatever material was handy at the time: cardboard, tar paper, left over scraps of wood. My Youth with a Mission (YWAM) [1] expedition into Mexico was truly memorable. I saw the smiles of the poor as they welcomed my wife, Debbie, and me into their humble houses. Most were the size of our garden shed at home. We were on an YWAM Discipleship Training School (DTS) [2] outreach.

Our first mission involved handing out clothing and bibles as we went door to door in this Mexican shantytown just over the El Paso, Texas border. Our initial intimidation was broken as the hospitality of the Mexican people overwhelmed us. Family after family graciously invited us in and asked us to sit down. Most places only had a bed. We did a lot of smiling because we knew only a few phrases in Spanish like, "We are Christians from Canada; we have a free gift for you; do you have a Bible in your home; can we pray for you?" At the end of the day I felt great! I was doing missionary work: giving out Bibles and tracts, helping the needy and praying for the sick. I thought to myself, "Lord, You are so good! Here I am with my wife and two children, Karl, seven at the time, and Karin, four years old, on a mission trip to Mexico." This was a wonderful learning experience for our family. Little did I know how much the Lord was about to teach us.

Walking back along the dirt roads, our excitement level grew as we saw the crowd milling around our team's parked school bus. It looked like the whole village had come to see us off. With children clamoring all over us, we did our best to pack up and give our final farewell hugs. I went to grab our carry-on bag that I had left under the school bus seat that morning. Not finding it, I assumed my wife had picked it up. Everything we had of value was in that bag: our passports, driver's license and the $80.00 we had as spending money for the next two months. "It has to be under one of the seats!" exclaimed Debbie. "Surely one of our team had moved it to a secure place," I nervously assured her. A thorough search came up with *nada*.

My earlier exhilaration turned to despair as I thought of the ramifications to all of this. With no passports we could be detained at the Mexico/US border. I had no driver's license or identification. We were left with no money for two months. We had known that the $80.00 was not enough in the first place, but we stepped out in faith believing the Lord was going to somehow provide more for us. My frustrations turned silently toward God. "Lord, here we are doing mission's work; we gave out all day and now we have been robbed by the same people we were trying to help! We might not even be able to get out of this stinking country plus we have no money! I am one of the bus drivers but now I have no license. I guess our mission trip is over!" I was glad no one could hear my inward ranting. I called out to God, *but the heavens were as brass.* [3] God was silent. I just hate it when He does that!

As we inched our way through downtown Juarez rush hour, I felt this enveloping darkness; it was as though the hordes of Hell had been unleashed against us. I just wanted to get back to our YWAM base in El Paso, and then this acrid smell of smoke started to permeate the air. Our bus caught fire. I could not believe what was going on! Panic set in as our team of thirty-five young adults scrambled out of the bus. Now, not only did I not have identification or money; our vehicle was on fire! My earlier, "Life is great," feeling was no longer even a memory. My kids were crying; my wife… was ready to push the ejection seat if there was one. Our first day in Mexico had turned into a bad movie.

My only anchor of hope was that I knew God had called us to this. A glimmer of faith started to rise deep within me as I reflected upon the journey that got us here in the first place.

— — —

Magician to Missionary

Life took on a whole new dimension for me the evening back in May of 1979 when I got on my knees and whole heartedly said, "Yes, Jesus. I will follow you." You can read about this incredible transformation from Magician to Missionary in my book *Come Follow Go*. [4]

It did not take me long to venture out on my first missionary journey. My best friend, Stew Motteram, was not happy with my newfound religion, as he called it. I had no desire to carry on with my former decadent lifestyle. But I did need to talk to Stew. Bible in one hand and a case of beer in the other, I proceeded to his house. I do not recommend this form of evangelism, but my reasoning was sincere. I figured that a case of beer would get me into his house.

Stew looked aggravated as I sat in his living room. He knew way more about the Bible and Christianity than I did, so proceeded to pepper me with questions all night long.

My main response was, "I do not know the answer to that one either. All I know is that whatever happened on the inside of me–you need!" I am sure we were both frustrated with each other that evening.

A few days later sitting in my living room, we were at it again, this time fumbling through the scriptures. "Read that again," he asked. Mark 11:24 *"Whatever things you ask when you pray, believe that you receive them, and you will have them."* "That is it," he cried out, "I asked for salvation, and now I just need to receive it! I have got it! I already have it!" This was such a revelation to him that he literally fell out of his chair. We had experienced our first revival meeting and did not even know it.

My wife, Debbie, also came to know the Lord around the same time. We were both very zealous for the things of God. In His wonderful wisdom, the Lord knew that our zeal needed to be balanced with an equal amount of wholeness and maturity.

For the next two years we were active members of Victoria Church of the Way. We were blessed to have Dr. Doug Roberts as our first pastor. Debbie and I were also mentored by assistant pastors of the church, Fred and Janet Farren. They are a wonderful, godly couple who we still look to as our spiritual mom and dad.

After two wonderful years at Church of the Way, Debbie and I sensed that a change was coming for us. We were willing to do anything and go anywhere.

Our church sponsored a missionary family in Honduras. While they were on their furlough, back in Victoria, Debbie and I got to know them a little and became intrigued with their missionary lifestyle. We started talking about the possibility of moving to Central America and working with this family. There was a strong sense within us that God was calling us to the mission field. We thought, perhaps, this was the change that was coming for us.

God was calling us to missions, but He also knew we needed more life-skill's training. Instead of traveling south we ended up moving four hours north to Campbell River, where we served as youth leaders with Fred and Janet Farren at Church of the Way.

Although we were heading north, we knew that God would eventually move us south. The prospects of being missionaries lingered in our hearts. I just did not think it was going to take twenty six years before we stepped upon Central American soil. In the meantime, we continued our discipleship training.

Keith Green

Our first mission's opportunity came two years after we had moved to Campbell River. Debbie and I were attending a Keith Green memorial concert in January of 1984.

I was captivated by Keith Green when I first heard him at a Jesus Northwest conference in 1979. There was something about the way he spoke that cut to the heart. He preached with zeal and boldness and lived a lifestyle to match. I loved his piano playing music style but even more the heart of passion that resonated in his lyrics. In July, 1982, Keith was killed in a tragic plane crash along with two of his children - Josiah, 3 and Bethany, 2. His wife, Melody was left with one year old Rebekah. She was also pregnant with their fourth child, Rachel.

Not long after his death, Melody shared at memorial concerts, throughout North America, about Keith's final message on the call to missions.

As Debbie and I sat in a crowd of thousands at the Agrodome arena in Vancouver, BC, Keith Green's final videotaped message gripped our hearts. *"This generation of Christians is responsible for this generation of souls on the earth,"* he said. *"I don't want to see us stand before God one day and say, 'But God, I didn't hear You call me.' Well, you don't need to hear a call. You're already called! In fact, if you stay home from going into all nations, you'd better be able to say to God, 'You called me to stay home, Lord, I know that for a fact!"*

Keith shared how he had recently returned from some overseas missionary bases and how his life had not been the same. *"Besides showing me how small my vision had been, God gave me a burden to see the ranks of His army in the fields swell!"*

I saw how evangelized my own country was, while the rest of the world was barely reached. I thought of the millions who needed the Gospel shown to them – yet hardly anyone was reaching them. As I spoke with missionaries and read statistics, I was shocked – I'd never known how little the need was being met!

15

When I returned home, I met with different leaders and studied God's Word to see what He said about reaching the lost in other countries.

Keith had a burning desire in his heart to see 100,000 young people released to the mission field over the next five years! Before his vision could materialize, he died at the age of 28.

After listening to this black and white message about the call to missions, delivered by this politically incorrect, piano-playing prophet, Debbie and I knew that God was stirring something in our hearts. On our way home from the concert we knew that it was time for us to step unto the mission field. We told the Lord that we were willing to go, wherever he would send us. We studied several mission agency brochures and felt impressed that God wanted us to train with Youth with a Mission.

Knowing God's call can be likened to a boat anchored in a harbour. As the tide goes in and out or the winds increase we have an assurance that our boat will not drift away. We may not see the anchor under the water, but can feel the tug as it holds our boat steady.

As our YWAM school bus was filling up with smoke, I felt the tug of our anchor. Even though we had just been robbed, I knew that months before we had let out our anchor. We were going to be ok, because God had called us to this mission's adventure.

So there we were, robbed and broken down in Mexico, holding unto the call of Jesus to go and make disciples of all nations. I knew we were in the right place, even though it felt like all Hell was trying to discourage us from continuing. God had sent us, and I knew that He was with us!

Our mechanics fixed the fire problem. There had been an electrical short somewhere under the dash. We made it across the border even though we had no identification. What happened next humbled me. That evening our team took a love offering for our family. We ended up with over $250.00 US funds to replace the $80.00 we had lost. The following day our group returned to the Juarez dump. As our team filed out of the bus, I saw a little barefoot boy running towards us. With a big smile on his face, he presented us with our carry-on bag. The only thing missing was a twenty-dollar bill. After a fair bit of repentance on my part, I was ready to do missions.

Chapter 2

<u>Shot Gun Approach</u>

"The Bible is not the basis of missions;
missions is the basis of the Bible"
Ralph Winter, missiologist

Preaching the gospel in Mexico is easy. I initially discovered this on our YWAM outreach and then during my early days of leading mission teams from our church in Canada to Tijuana. We went into all kinds of Mexican villages and town squares, where we would set up our sound system and invite people to a special meeting. "Come, the Canadians are here! We have a special program for children and adults. Come hear the music and see the dramas." Our music team would begin and people would start to come.

The younger children were always the first to arrive and then came the moms toting their babies. I found that a small crowd always gathers a larger crowd. After 30 minutes we would be surrounded, many times, by hundreds of curious onlookers. After many vibrant and lively Spanish worship choruses, a few testimonies and drama presentations, someone from the team would close with an altar call.

I would usually ask, "How many here today have sinned? Raise your hand." Most of the people would respond. I would share, "If you did not raise your hand, I know you are not telling the truth. The Bible declares that all have sinned and have fallen short of the glory of God. Let us try that again. How many standing here today can honestly say that they have sinned? Some of you need to raise both hands." This time hands would go up everywhere. "How many want to be free from their sin, totally clean, as though you had never sinned?" Again, a sea of hands would wave in the air at the offer. The gospel truly is good news! I would conclude by sharing, "We are here today with a message from God. The songs we have sung, the testimonies you have heard and the dramas you have witnessed all point to a God who is so loving that He sent Christians all the way from Canada to share this good news with you."

After the group had fully understood the gospel message, I would move right to the third question, "How many here today are willing to humble yourselves, as sinners in desperate need of cleansing, and call upon Jesus, the Saviour, to be Lord of your life?" I stress the monumental and eternal significance of this question. "God is looking for those who are absolutely sincere and ready to make a 100% wholehearted turnaround. If you have never responded to this good news offer before, come forward now."

Normally it does not take long for many of the villagers to come forward and kneel in the dirt. I share with them that what they are about to go through is like a marriage ceremony. "You are about to make a decision that will change your life forever, but it is only the first step into a lifelong relationship with the living God." As I conclude I welcome them as brothers and sisters in the Lord. This is worth the long and tedious drive south! I have discovered that there is nothing more fun and exhilarating than preaching the gospel and seeing people come forward to become genuine followers of Jesus.

Loving Confrontation

It was not until about my fourth trip that the Lord, lovingly and tenderly, confronted me. "So, John, what is happening with the thousand or so people, over the last couple of years, who have come forward at your altar calls?" As I pondered the question, I was not sure what He was getting at, so I replied, "Is there something wrong with getting people saved?" He then referred me to the "great commission" found in Matthew 28. "Go ye and make disciples of all nations, teaching them…" He shared with me that I had done a marvellous job at the "go ye" part, but the main focus of His final charge to His followers was to make disciples.

One of the drawbacks to short term missions can be leading people to salvation without providing follow-up discipleship. I was guilty of this when we first started. I was practicing evangelism without any potential for discipleship. I would drive our teams around looking for public parks or villages that were newly inhabited where we could set up, gather a crowd and preach the gospel. Getting people saved was easy and it was exhilarating. Unfortunately, since we did not connect with any of the local churches in those areas, we had no follow up in place for these new converts. I figured that God would take care of them.

My dilemma was seeing the overwhelming needs and opportunities in the Tijuana area. What used to be a small tourist town has grown to a population of over four million. My first response was to spread out and preach the gospel to as many people as possible. I call this the shot-gun method because our approach was scattered. After a while I realized that my efforts were only scratching the surface in comparison to the ever growing needs that I saw.

As I shared my frustrations with the Lord, His response to me was rather liberating. He told me that I was not called to reach the whole Tijuana mission field, but I did have a part to play. As a local church, I have realized that He has not called us to reach the whole world but instead wants us to focus on specific places. Together, as each part of the body of Christ does its share, the task of worldwide missions will be accomplished.

Since the loving rebuke and the words of liberation from the Lord, I began to remodel our approach to Short Term Missions. We intentionally became more focused. Rather than trying to reach the whole world we are focusing on specific areas and working closely with the district leaders and local pastors. I was learning.

After leading more than 40 missions teams from Canada to Mexico, I still had much to learn about how to incorporate the first part of the great commission "Go ye" into the second part "make disciples." For this reason, I believe the Lord sent Debbie and me to Costa Rica.

Chapter 3

Mission Training 101

"The spirit of Christ is the spirit of missions. The nearer we get to Him the more intensely missionary we become."
Henry Martyn

Debbie and I knew we were called to missions back in 1980, early in our walk with the Lord. We approached our pastor, Dr. Doug Roberts, at the time sharing with him about our desire to be missionaries in Central America. He wisely advised us to plug into our local church, get some more training and wait for the Lord to open doors. Subsequently, rather than sending us south, the Lord moved us from our homeland, Victoria, north to Campbell River to work with pastors Fred and Janet Farren.

In 1984, the call to missions resurfaced. We sold everything and took our two young children with us for six months of Youth with a Mission discipleship training. Our desire for missions only intensified. I tried negotiating with the Lord about continuing on with YWAM but He said, "Go back and impart to the church what you have just learned."

Costa Rica

After 25 years of "training" (youth pastoring, overseeing a Christian school, pastoring a church and leading short term mission teams from Canada to Mexico) that early call to go south started to percolate in my heart. In 2005, I started to hear about Costa Rica everywhere. The call to go was resonating in my heart. I questioned and pondered this for a year. "Lord, we are well established as pastors now in Campbell River. I'm 56 years old. Shouldn't I be looking more at retirement than heading out as a missionary to a country I have never even visited? All of our family and friends are here; Why Costa Rica…Why not Mexico…Why this late in life?" I have discovered that the Lord does not always answer all of my questions, but He does assure me that I am heading in the right direction.

Pastor Barry McGaffin, our Canadian Foursquare mission's coordinator at the time, mentioned to us that there was an opportunity for a full time missionary couple to be sent out from the Canadian national church. This news certainly brought affirmation that indeed the Lord was preparing a way for us. Just like in the old "Get Smart" TV series where Maxwell Smart walks briskly ahead with doors opening before him, we felt the same way as we continued to pursue the Lord's will for our lives. He was putting all the pieces together.

In February of 2006, Debbie and I were sent for some mission's training at Foursquare Missions International (FMI) in Los Angeles and then in May we visited Costa Rica for two weeks to scout out the land and make sure that we had a clear "yes" to leave everything familiar and move to Central America. We met with FMI missionaries, Lewie and Linda Richey, who were serving in Costa Rica at the time. They graciously welcomed us and helped us to get connected with some of the Foursquare leaders in the country. We were treated like dignitaries. We got to experience much of the culture and living conditions. We saw the beauty and the bugs, the highways and the by ways, the beaches and the poverty. After two weeks of visiting churches, driving around the country and staying in the homes of everyday Costa Rican people, the "yes" became "YES!"

I vividly remember the flood of emotions and thoughts that almost overwhelmed me as our plane was getting ready to land at the San Jose, Costa Rica national airport on November 15, 2006. "This is not a short term mission trip. You don't get to go back in two weeks. You have left family, friends, ministry and everything familiar to go somewhere absolutely foreign to you. You don't know anybody nor do you know the language. Are you sure you know what you are doing?" I could well relate to Abraham, as it says in Hebrews 11:8: "*And he went out, not knowing where he was going.*" We were the foreigners coming in not knowing where we were going, the aliens landing where culture and language and infrastructures are radically different from what we have so been used to. Again, I could feel the tug of the anchor that even though I was not sure what I was doing or where I was going; I was with the One who did. This perspective has been the basis of our Christian life.

I am so happy to be part of a church family that has given us the liberty to pursue the will of God for our lives. Our Canadian Foursquare family has released us to follow His mission for us in Costa Rica. After eight months of language training, the only directive we had was to head west to the province of Guanacaste. The Costa Rican Foursquare leaders felt that this was an area that had the greatest need for establishing more churches. We felt it strategic to be close to Liberia, the capital of the province, as well as to be fairly close to the Nicaraguan border. The doors opened up for us to settle into the beach community of Playas del Coco which is about 45 minutes from Liberia. Nicaragua is another 45 minutes north.

Amazing Fish Story

Early one morning during my prayer time at the beach, I was in my usual place over on the right side of Playas del Coco, when all of a sudden a huge school of small fish swarmed in. The water was absolutely teeming with fish and then as the waves were washing in, some of the fish started to come up on the land and were trapped onshore. I thought to myself, "Fishing with Jesus is easy!" So there I was rescuing these fish and throwing them back in the water. As this was happening the Lord spoke to me that as I continue to go out, He will bring about the people to harvest. He also showed me that as I was rescuing fish, if there was no one to throw them back into the water they would have been trapped and would have died. So it is with people in this world. There are many who have been trapped on the shores of life and need someone to help them into the living waters.

Now comes the incredible part. Later on that afternoon, as I was heading off to my daily time of sharing with people in the downtown area, I started talking with one of the laborers across the street from where we were living. He found out that I was a Christian and invited me to share with some of the other workers who lived in very rustic conditions in the back of the condo complex they were working on. About fifteen Nicaraguan men showed up, so I simply shared who I was, an ambassador for the King of Kings. I asked if any of them had a Bible. Only one did so I started handing out New Testaments. I ran out so I told them I would be back in five minutes with more.

When I got home I quickly loaded up on Bibles, more gospel information and grabbed my guitar. After my speedy return, I started to lead them in a few Spanish worship songs that I had been working on.

While we were singing ten more men showed up. I figured this was a good time to preach the gospel. After sharing with them a clear and full presentation, they all openly, eagerly and willingly knelt in the rubble of the construction lot to receive prayer. While this was happening more men showed up. I shared with them that I was looking for disciples to disciple so that they could learn to go and make more disciples. After the meeting, they said that more men needed to hear about this so they invited me to come for lunch the next day and to bring more Bibles and gospel literature.

Debbie made a good batch of cookies to take over to them that next morning. We had never met people so hungry for God. They asked us to continue every Sunday afternoon at 2:00 pm when they got off work. Debbie and I were very excited about what the Lord had in store. We had always felt that God wanted us, as well, to minister in Nicaragua. Now he was bringing the Nicaraguans to us. Out of this encounter, we started our first Foursquare Church of Nicaragua in Costa Rica on a construction lot across from where we were living. The picture above shows this group. On my right is Pastor Juan Zepeda who has been overseeing our church in Martina Bustos since 2009. I am the white guy in the back row.

For the next few months we continued to hold services on Sunday afternoons and Wednesday evenings with our Nicaraguan workers. We started to really bond with these men. Even though our language skills were still limited, the Lord showed us that we could still communicate our love for them in practical ways. Every afternoon Debbie would make up ice cold lemonade to give out to the workers on the site. We were simply doing this because we honestly cared for the people who God had brought our way.

Missions 201

Our next step was missions training 201. I was sharing with our new disciples that being a follower of Jesus involved more than attending church services and Bible studies. Discipleship needs to be combined with evangelism. I felt impressed that it was time to take these guys on a short term mission's trip. Not knowing where to go, I took a day to go exploring to find a neighborhood that needed a church. There was no handbook on how to do this but I felt this tug in my heart to go to a small town called Filadelfia which is about a 30 minute drive from Playas del Coco.

After driving around the downtown area for a while, I found a little side road that edged along the Tempisque River and came upon a little barrio called La Isleta. Not sure what to do next, I parked my car and figured that maybe I should visit some of the homes in the area.

The people I met were very friendly. I found out that there was no church in this village, so that perked my interest. As soon as I came to the home of Isabella I knew that this was the place. She was a widow in her sixties, and had lived in this house along the river for the past thirty years. As I sat on her front porch I felt like I was with family. She was very welcoming and said that by all means we could have church meetings at her house. I had found the person of peace in the community.

Jesus mentioned this to His disciples when He sent them on a short term mission trip. He gave them very clear and simple instructions. Luke 10:5-7: *"But whatever house you enter, first say, 'Peace to this house.' And if a son of peace is there, your peace will rest on it; if not, it will return to you. And remain in the same house, eating and drinking such things as they give, for the laborer is worthy of his wages. Do not go from house to house."*

Since that time, all of the dozen or so houses along that section of the river have been removed because of the seasonal flood problems in the area. The house of peace is the only one that still remains.

The following Sunday we borrowed a van plus used our seven passenger Hyundai Galloper to transport our Nicaraguan disciples to start our first church service on the porch at Isabella's house in La Isleta.

Now we had two churches to work with: our group of Nicaraguan workers in Playas del Coco and new church members in La Isleta. I was learning about the simple mission of following Jesus.

The secret truly starts with coming to Him, which leads us to be able to follow Him and to go where He sends us.

Serving on the field as full time missionaries for eight years, Debbie and I also had the honor of receiving forty short term mission teams from Canada and the USA plus we led five mission teams of Costa Ricans to minister in Nicaragua. In our thirty one years of being involved with missions, sending and receiving teams, we have learned a few things along the way. I write this book with the hope of encouraging local churches to continue to send out missionaries, short and long term. I believe that

Short Term Missions teams can be effective and make a long term impact upon the communities that they are reaching out to. For this to happen there are some perspectives that need to be changed and methods to be adjusted. The remainder of this book will tackle some of the mistakes that have been made, but always with the heart that we can learn from our mistakes. As I have mentioned in the previous chapters, I have made mistakes. I have needed some attitude adjustments but, all along, the lord has been very gracious and patient to lead me and to show me better ways to make a long term impact with short term mission teams. Let me begin by addressing twelve ingredients that are necessary for teams to implement if they are serious about making a long term impact.

I present these with a hope and a desire to see a future movement of mission teams that will be able to work towards longer term results.

Chapter 4

Top Twelve Ingredients for Long Term Impact

"If God calls you to be a missionary, don't stoop to be a king"
Jordan Grooms [5]

I thoroughly enjoy the smell and taste of fresh baked bread. Knowing that my hands worked the dough somehow makes it even tastier. As long as I follow the directions and use the proper ingredients I can open the oven door and marvel at the outcome of my baking skills. In the same way, the success of a short term mission trip depends very much upon the ingredients that go into the trip itself. I have found that the following twelve components are important and should be considered as part of the recipe for a mission trip that has the potential to make a long term impact.

1). A team should come to do ministry in partnership with churches rather than doing ministry for churches.

I could not see my attitude of superiority until the Lord asked me to picture myself as a Mexican pastor. The Lord asked, "How would you feel, John, if a rich Norwegian team showed up, unannounced, and decided to take over your church in Canada for a few days? They have heard about how the Canadian church has struggled and want to help you fix it. They have brought some good Norwegian worship songs translated into English. They are ready to put on a Vacation Bible School but the material is in Norwegian and so will need to be translated. They have a group of 20 people, half of them youth and only two of them speak English. They need a place to stay for free, with cheap food and warm showers if possible. During the trip some of the group's energy will be spent on resolving tension between team members. They would like you to arrange some sightseeing for them on their free day. Do you want them to come?"

I immediately saw the folly of my ways. So many times I had shown up ready to preach, teach, lead worship, evangelize, and do children's ministry without considering the feelings of the local church pastor we had come to bless. We had come to serve but unknowingly took over. It was like coming into someone's home and starting to rearrange the furniture to our liking.

Our goal is not to ride into town as though we have all the answers to their problems, but to go with a heart to serve and the disposition of a learner, with the humility to take our cues from national leaders. If we can build a level of trust, the most effective trips will be extensions of another church's ministry.

At a pastor's conference in Tijuana I realized that I needed to apologize to the many pastors attending for the many times I have barged in rather than respectfully asking if we could be of any assistance. I also encouraged them to be a little more assertive in dealing with teams coming in.

When your short term ministry team leaves a particular setting, it is important to understand that Christians will still live and work where you visited. Your desire should be to serve at the request of and under the direction of local church leadership. Since they have a long term vision for their community, your mission trip can be part of the process of helping to make a long term impact. For example, if the local church has a vision to reach the homeless and is involved with street ministry, perhaps your team could prepare to help them out in this area.

I am discovering more and more that missions is not about us going to do something for the people of Central America or where ever, but building relationship with them and partnering with them. Doing things with people, not for people should be our motto. Always.

Along this same line, I believe that it is important to communicate directly with the missionaries your church supports and trusts, to find out whether they would like a team to come and work with them. These missionaries can also provide helpful feedback that comes from experience and understanding of the culture and needs in the area. Just make sure they feel the freedom to say no and dictate the details of the trip, such as how many people should come. I heard of a missionary who asked for eight people, and the church responded by sending more than 100 youth. We need to listen! If your church does not support long term missionaries, I would suggest doing so along with your short term cross-cultural ministry.

2). Teams should come prepared to share more than just a salvation message.

We have had many teams that come and do their presentations from church to church trying to get their salvation message out to as many people as possible, not realizing that most church members have already heard this message over and over again from other teams or ministers who have been there before, let alone from the local church pastors and visiting speakers.

Visiting teams should be aware that they are not the only ones sharing the gospel. The local churches that I work with are very active in reaching out to their communities. Evangelizing a city, region or nation is a long term endeavor that involves committed long-term pastors, missionaries and lay leaders. We appreciate teams coming alongside of us but they should also be realistic about what can be accomplished during a one week short term mission outreach.

If your purpose is to minister in churches, please come with presentations that will help encourage and motivate the local church members. For this reason teams should prepare more than just a salvation message. Obviously, I am not discouraging teams to come ready to share the gospel, but let us also bring messages on forgiveness, healing and deliverance etc.

A team from Beausejour Canada, led by pastors Chris and Liza Jordan, came with a very effective and simple presentation called "Cardboard Testimonies." As the team members came forward, they each held a piece of cardboard in front of them. On one side was briefly written something they had struggled with: "Rejected at birth"… "Fearful and shy growing up"…"Always tried to prove myself" etc. On the other side was written how the Lord had healed or freed them up. "God has always loved me"…"Through Him, I can do all things"… "Set free to be me"…etc.

This made room for people in the congregations to identify with similar problems and provided opportunities for heart felt testimonies from the team and powerful prayer ministry times with the members of the church who were there.

If your team wants to focus on evangelism, ask if you can bring your presentations to schools, rehab centers, prisons, and local parks where people hang out. For most of these you will need to apply for permission or permits beforehand and so you need to have people on the field who can prepare the way for your group to come.

As I will discuss in the following chapter, to make a long term impact, evangelism needs to be combined with discipleship. Evangelism, on its own, does not produce long term disciples. Discipleship, on its own, will not produce more disciples if we are not going out to find them. Without evangelism, discipleship is simply incomplete. The reality is that we need to pursue both.

3). Teams should take time in relating to the people and the culture.

An innocent mistake that I see mission teams make is focusing on those who are going and not on those who are receiving the teams. We send youth so they can have an experience or so God can really capture their hearts.

I hope this does not sound harsh, but as we send mission teams, we truly need to be honoring to God by loving the people in the countries where we are going, not just using them for some "experience" for our team members. Experiences will come and they are important but should be a byproduct of our reason to go.

Being on the field full time has helped us to understand the importance of developing meaningful relationships with our leadership team and valuable opportunities to not only teach but to be an example to them. We try to instill this with people coming to partner with us as well.

Encourage your team to spend time with locals. Make sure nationals are fully involved in your visit and follow their lead. If you are working on a project together, ask your national co-workers to teach you. If you have a skill they could use, ask if they would like to learn it. Ask questions about the lives and problems of the people you meet. Learning from the people of the country you visit will give you an understanding of the country that a foreigner cannot give.

One of our latest teams from Courtenay, Canada truly demonstrated this value of relationship building by coming to honor the pastors whom we are working with. The team provided a delicious Canadian salmon lunch. I knew that the majority of our church pastors had never tasted salmon before. The team also supplied some great Christian books in Spanish for each leader, along with a nice gift bag. The part that impacted our group the most was when the Canadians offered to wash their feet and to pray over them. The best way I could describe it was to say that the tears were flowing. I think if Jesus went on a mission trip, He would have done the same.

The vital part of this is that it set the tone for ministering together that week. When the team came to minister at one of our churches they already had established a relationship with the pastors by honoring them, serving them and washing their feet. I truly saw the Lord give favor to this team as they ministered. It was like the heavens had been opened as God honored those who honored Him.

Matthew 25:40 *"Truly I say to you, Inasmuch as you did it to one of the least of these My brothers, you have done it to Me."*

During our time in Costa Rica, the Lord has lovingly showed me that people and relationships and greetings are really important. I have learned the importance and value of sitting on a porch, simply spending time with the family. I generally need to share with visiting mission teams that when we arrive at a work project, our first task is to greet the Costa Rican people, before unloading the tool box.

I believe the best approach for arriving teams, is to initially have a fellowship time with the pastor and his congregation, and have the pastor share his vision. The visiting leader can then introduce the team, share their vision for coming and then seek ways to partner together in the work of the ministry.

On the other end of this spectrum, it is important to involve your whole congregation. When I sent teams from our church in Campbell River, Canada we purposed to do missions together. I recognized the need for a strong support base of intercessors. If people could not go on the trip, many helped out financially or practically by contributing supplies for health kits or special gifts for children. There was a strong sense that we were about our Father's business: together in the harvest.

4). Teams should have the perspective that they are on His mission trip.

Short term mission trips have taught me a lot about myself. I have discovered that my motivations for doing missions have not been all that pure. I have been amazed at how easily my carnal nature can rise up and entwine itself in the service of the Lord. Hidden within my quest for souls, has also been this tinge of an appetite for numbers saved rather than the people themselves. I have discovered that it feels good to hand out clothing and food to the needy. It feels good to be thronged by children reaching for the toys you are about to give out. It feels good to see a group of 150 people come forward to accept Jesus as their Lord and Savior.

Although, it feels good to serve the Lord, I have learned that my motives can be subtly self-serving.

It would be good for those who will be bringing short term teams to Mexico, for example, to back up and make sure that their plans to send teams are well thought through in the broad perspective of their overall missions program, whether it be at the local church level or at the regional or denominational level. We have heard of some groups for whom their trip is just one more activity on the summer youth schedule: Knott's Berry Farm, Summer Camp, and Mexico.

Proverbs 19:12 is a verse that has much to tell us regarding many short term efforts, *"It is not good to have zeal without knowledge, not to be hasty and miss the way."* So many groups that come abound in zeal, but sadly are lacking in knowledge because they have not "done their homework," and end up missing the way. It is all too common for mission teams to come with the attitude of a teacher who has the answer to the problems before they play the role of a student to find out what the specific problems and needs are.

To combat this, it is important to understand that we are not going on our mission trip. God is the source of mission. It is not my mission; it is His mission. The church is rooted in the concept of the *Missio Dei,* which recognizes that there is one mission and it is God's mission. The word *missio* literally means sent. The church is not an end in itself; the church is sent into the world to fulfill the mission of God. In recognizing this, I have learned to be well prepared and yet totally flexible because we are on God's mission trip not mine. Mission is not a response to human need but a pursuit of the purposes of God.

Good missionaries are good students and respectful, sensitive guests in the countries where they serve. Seek out opportunities to learn as well as to teach, to listen as well as to speak, to observe as well as to do.
Would it not be great if the purpose of our team was to be an answer to the prayers of church members, and pastors who we will be reaching out to? We are not going with our own agenda. We should be going to serve and help meet the needs of the Body of Christ in the city or nation that God is sending us to. Our objective will motivate us to work alongside the local Christians and assist in bringing light into dark places. Our primary goal is to be a blessing to all those we work with.

Sometimes teams can get stuck in relief work or trying to meet needs. We paint, build, clean up neighborhoods and give out presents and do this because almost anyone in our churches can get involved and it makes us feel good.

One of the problems faced by North American teams is that we come from a results-oriented culture that feels like we are not making a difference unless we have something tangible that we can point to and say, "Look at what we did!"

If you want to embrace short term missions with a long term impact this area of coming to do relief work needs to take on some changes. Do not misunderstand: I am not talking about emergency relief situations. I am talking about long-term care.

If your team comes to do something for someone that they can do themselves, this is not creating a long term impact. For example, I thought it was a great idea for visiting teams to come and clean up the neighborhood around our local church in Las Lomas in Playas del Coco. One of the reasons that I thought it was a great idea was because everyone on the team could participate, and it gave an opportunity to work alongside members of the local church. After many attempts at cleaning up this barrio I see little long term impact. I am sure the Canadians could say to themselves, "Hey, look at what we did! We cleaned up the neighborhood. We made this a better place to live." Unfortunately, after the team leaves for Canada and as I drive into the community a few days later I see that the garbage has returned to the streets. What did we end up with? Short term mission makes short term impact. The problem with many trips is that we perpetuate relief instead of moving toward development work.

How can we make more of a long term impact? Communities like Las Lomas have learned that when a charitable organization comes in and does everything for the local community, then they only end up creating a dependence on our help.

The solution is more about creating opportunities for the local communities to own these projects. The jobs, the education, and the responsibility are all essential elements to helping developing nations break the cycle of poverty. This does not mean that we need to stop showing up, but it does mean that we need to rethink what we do when we get there.

Instead of doing work for them, why not help them to organize a community clean-up campaign and participate with them rather than coming to do it for them.

Relief is appropriate for short periods, but if we want to get involved in alleviating physical poverty and use that platform to share the gospel and relieve spiritual poverty, we must move toward development work. It is harder, takes longer, but is certainly a better form of mercy and justice ministry.

This type of ministry then is better served in coordination with the full time missionary in the area and the local church members. Using the simple example of the Las Lomas neighborhood clean-up project, it would be far more impactful if the team came to work with the people who live in the neighborhood than do the work for the neighborhood. After working with the neighbors on a project, it can then provide a platform for the team to share the good news.

This is a simple example but I believe can be applied to many areas of practical service in our communities.

One of the temptations of people on a short-term mission trip is to become overwhelmed by what appears to be poverty when looking at the rest of the world from their perspective. Here it is helpful to distinguish between absolute and relative poverty. People living in absolute poverty most likely will need outside assistance or they will not survive. This help may need to be given in the form of medicine, food, shelter or the like. Relative poverty— the kind many mission teams encounter—means that people may not be as well off as they are, but they are quite capable of surviving in the society and surroundings where God has placed them. Those who live in relative poverty are often susceptible to the kind of dependency we should all seek to avoid. It is easy to give people the impression that since their houses or church buildings are not as good as ours, they need financial assistance for an upgrade. When outsiders give that impression to the person living in relative poverty, local people may begin to long for something they did not know was a need. As one church leader in Uganda said, "We did not know we were poor until someone from the outside told us." Short-term missionaries should be reminded that their compassion must not result in doing for others what they can and should do for themselves. Sometimes the difficulty is knowing where the line is drawn between absolute and relative poverty. Leaders of short-term mission groups would do well to reflect on issues such as this before undertaking a short-term trip.

The book *Toxic Charity* by Robert D. Lupton shares openly how churches and charities can hurt those they help and how to reverse it. It takes a candid and sometimes critical look behind the scenes at the unintended harm inflicted by our kindness. The author has provided a checklist of criteria that can help us determine which actions should be undertaken when we want to help others. It is like an "Oath for Compassionate Service" to guide us toward providing responsible and effective aid.

The Oath for Compassionate Service

- Never do for the poor what they have (or could have) the capacity to do for themselves.
- Limit one-way giving to emergency situations.
- Strive to empower the poor through employment, lending, and investing, using grants sparingly to reinforce achievements.
- Subordinate self-interests to the needs of those being served.
- Listen closely to those who seek to help, especially to what is not being said---unspoken feelings may contain essential clues to effective service.
- Above all, do no harm.

Here in Costa Rica, we are surrounded by a multitude of needs. The problem with the need is that the need is never finished. I have discovered that if I am not careful the need will finish me before I finish with its demands. I need to be careful to not allow the need to begin to set my agenda. There are many voices out there calling for my time that are trying to rise above the voice of my Master.

When you study the life of Jesus you will see that He never allowed the need or the opportunity to set the agenda for his ministry. While Christian mission invariably responds to human need, ultimately it is the reality of God's initiative and purpose that needs to be the basis of what we do. We need to do missions from God's perspective and His directive.

I have learned that simply trying to meet practical needs in the mission fields of Tijuana, Mexico or Filadelfia, Costa Rica is not going to the heart of what those cities need. God did not call me to try to fix the overwhelming practical needs in Costa Rica. He called me to preach the gospel. I believe that this should be the focus of our short term mission trips as well. Preaching the gospel has great potential for long term impact.

5). Teams should refer to those who have boots on the ground.

The churches that Debbie and I have been working with have been blessed by teams coming in to help with building renovations and so I am not opposed to groups coming to help in practical ways. The important aspect that I see is that we need to do it in conjunction with the missionaries who have boots on the ground and the local church leaders involved. There needs to be open and honest dialogue between the sending churches and those on the receiving end.

This is another reason why it is so important for visiting mission teams to refer beforehand to those who are full time on the field. Otherwise, you can get houses in Latin America that have been painted over and over again by different short-term teams. I also heard about the well-meaning teams who rushed to Honduras to help rebuild homes destroyed by Hurricane Mitch and spent on average $30,000.00 per home. If they had referred to the local leaders they would have found out that typical homes could have been built for $3,000.00 each.

When teams come in with an agenda, it is difficult for the directors of an orphanage to say, "We have another suggestion on how your team could invest your money." Instead, they welcome the church mission group to come and paint knowing that the money spent to cover the costs of their Central America mission's trip would have been enough to hire two local painters and two new full-time teachers and purchase new uniforms for every student in the school.

Our Costa Rican brothers and sisters are often reluctant to give us the frank feedback we need to hear, so I have discovered that we need to work hard to show them that we really want to hear how we can do things better.

As on the field missionaries, Debbie and I were in touch with the real needs around us. As well, the local church pastors, whom we were working with, are in touch with the real needs of their communities. I remember several times where I have gone with teams to distribute food supplies to homes in the community of Martina Bustos. This is one of the more humble areas that we are working in where there is no running water to the homes and many families live without electricity. Everyone there would appreciate a little extra food and so I figured it was fine to distribute what we had to everyone we visited. When I came with 30 grocery bags to distribute, Pastor Juan Zepeda asked me if we were giving food to everyone we visited? I explained that yes, this was our idea. I noticed a little bit of concern in his voice when he mentioned that he knew of some specific families that could really use some help.

I realized that even though I was the area missionary; he knew the families of his community, and like a caring shepherd he wanted to reach out to those who were truly in need. I used to give out groceries as we visited families door to door to share the gospel with them. I would mention that the donation of food was to show God's love in a practical way. I know everyone who received was thankful but the impact we were making was minimal. I realize now that the money we spent to purchase 30 small food bags and given out randomly could have been better invested to purchase 10 full sized grocery bags and given out to families that really needed help.

Over our eight years in Costa Rica we have only had one team approach us with a desire to build a small house for a needy family, and when they did, I knew exactly the family to recommend. I have also seen the long term impact that this blessing has been to the family. They are very grateful to the Lord and have become solid and respected members of their local church.

It comes down to that whole realm of building relationships. The teams that have made the most long term impact have been those who have connected with one or two churches and have come back year after year to build upon those relationships. For the first mission trip we are visitors. When we meet again the second year we are becoming friends. After the third year we have become family.

6). Teams should do what Jesus would do.

I now approach door to door ministry more with the attitude of Apostle Peter. Acts 3:6 *But Peter said, "Silver and gold have I none, but what I have I give you."* The most important thing we have to offer is what Jesus sent His disciples out to give. Luke 9:2 *"And He sent them to proclaim the kingdom of God and to heal the sick."* As followers of Jesus, perhaps our approach to missions should be more in line with, "What would Jesus do?"

If Jesus were to lead your Short Term Mission team, how would He do it? What would He have you to do? Where would He take you? One of the main keys to making a long term impact is to allow Jesus to be Lord of your mission trip.

I long to see more short term mission teams come to minister in the fullness of the supernatural power of the Holy Spirit. Many of the people that they will be ministering to are held captive by the chains of sin that grip their lives. Others are living in sickness and are in need of an encounter with the message of hope and healing that is found in Jesus. The people they come into contact with need more than a story; they need to experience the power of God. If Jesus was the Lord of our mission trip, I am sure that He would still emphasize our need to preach the gospel of the Kingdom, to cast out demons and to heal the sick. These are three great ingredients for long term impact.

My exhortation is to be careful that you do not minimize what Jesus has called your mission team to do. Challenge your team to do what they naturally cannot do. If we can do it on our own, the reality is that we really do not need Jesus. A church led short term mission team is not simply a service group coming to do volunteer work. That can be part of the package but we have more to offer.

I emphasize this because I have seen and experienced far too much of the supernatural, wonderworking power of God in my life to be satisfied with a mere intellectual approach to the gospel.

Back in 1979, when I was a new Christian, I went to a meeting with Dennis and Rita Bennett at an Anglican church in Victoria, BC, Canada. During the Charismatic renewal of the late 1970's, Dennis, an Anglican minister, wrote an influential book about the baptism of the Holy Spirit called *Nine O'clock in the morning*. In the meeting he had people stand who needed healing and then the ones who were around them to lay hands on these people. This young lady was standing with hands raised in front of me, so I basically did what Dennis had asked and put my hand on this lady's back. I said some kind of feeble prayer and that was it. Dennis then asked for testimonies of people who were prayed for. This same lady, who I had laid my hands upon, immediately jumped to her feet and started proclaiming exuberantly how she felt this heat going up and down her spine and how, after many years of suffering, her back was pain free. I looked at my hand and thought to myself, "That certainly had nothing to do with me. I had no training or experience in healing, but God used me."

At the same meeting I saw people praying for this paralyzed lady in a wheelchair and thought to myself, "What are they doing?" This lady walked out of her wheel chair that night and is still walking today testifying of her miraculous healing. That was my first encounter with the healing power of God.

Shortly after this experience, after a Sunday morning service at Church of the Way in Victoria, I heard this commotion in the foyer and people gathering to look at what was going on. As I approached, I could feel a sense of evil permeating the air. In the corner of the entrance was a young man cowering like a wild animal. His fingers were horribly out stretched like claws and he was growling like a wolf in distress. I also saw the pastor and elders of the church with calmness and authority release him from his bondage.
After that experience I knew there was a devil and I saw the power of God come and set this person free.

Not that much later I was ministering at a prison and was with a small group of Christians from our church praying over this inmate who was heavily into transcendental meditation. I was still a very new Christian but was learning bible verses. In my zeal I proclaimed over him the scripture in Luke 10:19 *"Behold, I give to you authority to tread on serpents and scorpions, and over all the authority of the enemy. And nothing shall by any means hurt you."* He turned to look me in the eyes and with a loud, deep, ungodly voice he growled, "You have no power over me." Fear gripped the whole room. It certainly did me. I am thankful for our group leader who, with godly boldness, was able to speak love and truth to this man. After that experience I definitely knew there were demons because I just talked to one.

Around the same time, I was ministering to people lined up for prayer at our church service and I went to barely touch this lady on the shoulder when she falls to the ground and with hands stretched out towards me like claws she hissed, "Don't touch me!" I was thankful, again, for church leaders around me who were able to come and assist me.

The following week in a prayer line I put my hand on a person's head and they fell down. I had never seen this in church before. I thought I had killed somebody. I was definitely starting to see that there was an impartation of something going on as I laid hands on people.

I next saw the supernatural provision of God as I attended my first Christian conference, Jesus Northwest, 1979. My friend Stew Motteram and I spent all of our money traveling to the event but did not know it was going to cost $35.00 US for each of us to get in so we just kept moving forward in the lineup. As we approached the ticket counter, someone on the way out, held up two tickets and asked if anyone needed help getting in. We innocently raised our hands and in we went. We just thought that this was normal Christianity.

This next example showed me clearly how the supernatural world was closer to me than I realized. I was sitting in a huge foyer of a hotel in Toronto Canada when I saw, what looked like a homeless man, walk through the entrance doors far away on the other side of the room. As he sat down in a chair close to the doors, I sensed a compassion for this person and felt impressed by the Lord to go and talk to him. I waited a bit and then rose to get up. Immediately this man stood up, pointed his finger at me and said, "I don't want to talk with you," and walked out. Who told him that I wanted to talk with him?

I believe, as Christians, if we do not at least, once in a while, experience the supernatural power of God in our lives and in our church and during our mission trips, perhaps we should turn our license in.

This supernatural power of the Holy Spirit comes with a purpose: to preach the gospel, heal the brokenhearted, proclaim liberty, recovery of sight to the blind and to set the captives free. Jesus, Himself, made this very clear in Luke 4:18 *"The Spirit of the Lord is upon Me, because He has anointed me to preach the gospel to the poor; He has sent me to heal the brokenhearted, to proclaim liberty to the captives and recovery of sight to the blind, to set at liberty those who are oppressed."*

Genesis 49:22 *"Joseph is a fruitful bough, a fruitful bough by a well; His branches run over the wall."*

For me, this scripture out of Genesis is a wonderful word picture for missions: a fruitful church, sustained by a well, reaching over the wall. As churches, we are called, like Joseph, to extend our fruit bearing branches beyond the walls of our buildings to offer our fruit to those on the other side.

44

Clearly the fruit of a tree is not meant for the tree. Like an apple tree, the apples are not ripening so that the tree can receive and eat apples. The apples become ripe so that birds and people can enjoy and receive benefit from the fruit.

Unfortunately, there are churches that are full of apples but year after year the apples fall to the ground only for the members of the church to eat. Everyone thinks, "We have a big church with lots of apples. Look at the number of people we have! Look at the wonderful apples we have produced!" In reality, the members of this church have lost their purpose which is to extend themselves beyond the four walls of their sanctuary to offer their apples to those on the outside.

I have come to understand that the church *is* us, but it is not *for* us.

The "anointing" is not simply for us to bask in, and believe me I have done my share of carpet time, soaking in His presence and I value very much those intimate encounters with God. The baptism of the Holy Spirit is not for us to keep to ourselves, it has a purpose and that is to empower us to witness. Acts 1:8 *"But you shall receive power when the Holy Spirit has come upon you; and you shall be witnesses to Me in Jerusalem, and in all Judea and Samaria, and to the end of the earth."*

We are called to take the power of the Spirit with us on our short term mission trip.

7). Teams need to hold lightly to their plans in order to enable the Holy Spirit to guide them into His plans for their trip.

Acts 16:7 "They went as far as Mysia and tried to enter Bithynia, but the Spirit of Jesus did not let them."

After my Discipleship training school was over, in the spring of 1984, I was more than ready to continue on in the fast lanes of YWAM. The only problem I had was convincing the Lord that this was the perfect road for me and my family. The Lord's response was that I needed to go back to my local church. After my experience with YWAM, going back to the local church felt like getting off a jet ski to being stationed on a slow moving freighter. I really liked the exciting, fast pace and the close knit relationships that developed over our six months together.

The most difficult thing about my YWAM experience was the tearing away of well-established friendships as the 35 of us parted company. "Go back to Campbell River and integrate what you just learned into the ministry of your local church," was the clear directive I received from the Lord. It was not until four long years later that the Lord released me to venture out on our first short term mission's expedition.

Our team of ten, mostly teens from our Christian school, Life Christian Academy, was scheduled to leave on Boxing Day, 1988. For three months we prepared our skits, Spanish worship songs, and language skills. We were prayed up and pumped about going. A little over a week before we were set to go, my senior pastor, Fred Farren, came to me and said he had a real check about us going. He felt the timing was wrong.

My initial reaction was one of disbelief! "We have been preparing diligently for the past three months! We are prayed up, ready to go! We have a van and roof carriers that were purchased for this outreach! Everyone has their finances! This is a mission's trip! What could possibly be the problem?" Pastor Fred must have felt terrible about all of this, especially after listening to me, but he felt very strongly that we were not to go at this time.

The worst part was trying to explain this to our students. After a very tearful meeting we submitted ourselves to the direction of our leader. This turned out to be a valuable lesson for all of us. God, being omniscient, knew that starting on Boxing Day the Pacific Northwest would be hit with a major snow storm that would affect the entire highway system from British Columbia down to Northern California. Had we gone during that time, we would have faced extreme winter weather conditions.

Three months later we did leave for our first Mexico outreach and experienced the greatest adventure of our lives. I am so thankful for a leader that is tuned in to God and had the fortitude to stand up for his convictions. Even the Apostle Paul, on his missionary journeys, was clearly led by the Holy Spirit, and at times heard "No, I do not want you to go here or there."

Acts 16:6-7 *"Then they went through the region of Phrygia and Galatia because they had been prevented by the Holy Spirit from speaking the word in Asia. They went as far as Mysia and tried to enter Bithynia, but the Spirit of Jesus did not let them."*

I have learned, as well, to hold lightly to my plans. I usually come up with great itineraries outlining what I think we should be doing, but my plans do not always work well in Latin America. The Canadian clock, I have discovered, ticks a lot slower in Playas del Coco. Nobody is in a hurry to arrive at my scheduled meetings. The One we truly need to wait upon and give honor to at our meetings is the Holy Spirit. If He does not show up all we end up with is another meeting.

I have learned to be well prepared and yet totally flexible because we are on God's mission trip not mine. It is also a great experience for the team to learn how to listen for that still small voice of God's direction. I could write a book simply on the wonderful changes that God has brought to our itineraries. Let me share one.

Our plan for the day was to visit an orphanage, but I felt that God had more for us. I was not sure what God was up to so we loaded up the van and headed out. On our way we passed by an old church that I used to connect with.

Something happened at that church seven years prior that made me hesitant about stopping in, but I sensed the Lord wanted us to visit.

As Pastor Abdulio, of "Rey de Gloria" Foursquare Church, poked his head out the door to see who was calling, he looked rather despondent, although he tried to cheerfully greet the Canadian visitors. I was not planning to spend much time there but the Lord, as usual on these Mexico excursions, had other plans. Pastor Abdulio explained how the church had dwindled down to around twenty people and no matter how much they prayed there seemed to be some kind of hindrance to the Spirit of God moving in the place.

As we all joined hands in the sanctuary to pray for the pastor and the church, the Lord reminded me of the robbery that took place on the church grounds involving one of our Canadian teams. Pastor Stew Motteram and a group from his Full Gospel church in Quesnel were just beginning their ministry time at this place when they experienced the terror of being held up at gun point.

Two local banditos approached him with a gun held to his head and asked for the keys to their 15 passenger van. Stew's first reaction was to throw the keys into a large pile of garbage. As the keys went flying he heard a pop and total blackness set in. He figured, "Ok, I have been shot! So this is what death feels like." As he was waiting for the light at the end of the tunnel to materialize, he heard voices and then realized that the man with the gun had smashed the overhead light bulb and was making his getaway. Needless to say, this episode traumatized the team. Although they survived the ordeal, the trauma hindered them from proceeding on with their scheduled outreach.

As I mentioned this to our group, we all felt like we were touching upon something very significant. We asked the pastor if he would stand in the gap and ask forgiveness, on behalf of the Mexican robbers, to us the Canadians who were now there. Heaven broke lose as we prayed. Many in our group felt that a spiritual stronghold of terror had been broken over this church ministry. We then felt to displace the spirit of robbery by coming in the opposite spirit of giving, so our team took an offering from our personal finances and gave to this church. Afterwards, everyone remarked on the noticeable change in Pastor Abdulio. He was vibrant and alive and commented on the great weight that he felt was removed from his heart.

Obviously, my proposed trip to the orphanage was not happening that day, but I have learned to hold lightly to my plans so that the Lord can direct our steps. We ended up doing a service at "Rey de Gloria" that evening, as well as, ministering at their main service on Sunday morning.

I have experienced that the greatest opportunities for long term impact come when we intentionally submit our plans to the Lord and wait upon Him to lead us and to direct us during every day of our mission trip.

8). Team dynamics are important.

Unless you are highly organized, have great contacts on the ground and have years of experience in leading short term mission teams, I would lean towards smaller, higher quality teams. Group dynamics change significantly as the size of the group increases. With larger groups, the tendency is for a lot of the interaction to take place within the group itself, while smaller groups tend to interact more with the local people.

When it comes to team selection I suggest to keep the bar fairly high. Some churches, for example, will let virtually anyone in the youth group come who is willing and available. This may include non-Christians and some very marginal Christians, who can end up causing some real testimony problems when in the host country, especially if the host church was expecting a group of highly-committed Christians. It is also good to finalize the team roster well ahead of the trip. This helps insure everyone gets in on all the pre-trip training.

Every mission team is made up of individuals who have unique personalities, abilities and gifts, therefore every mission team is different. One of the key roles of a mission team leader is to discover the unique gifts and talents of the team and how to utilize the gift mix to create the most effective means by which the team can minister to others. The old navy expression, "all hands on deck" should be the expectation for mission team members. Let the singers sing, the prophets prophesy and the preachers preach, but everyone should come prepared to share a short testimony and to pray for people.

One of the benefits of a mission trip is that it does impact the lives of those going. This is a good thing. For me Missions was something I had to experience. Only then was I able to understand what Jesus said to His disciples, John 4:32 *"I have food you know nothing about."* As I mentioned before, to me, my first mission's trip was like being smitten with the mission bug. I got in touch with the very DNA of what we are called to. I have never recovered.

One of my best friends and subsequently my first convert, Stew Motteram, was the pastor of Lake View church in Quesnel, BC, Canada. I had been pulling on his shirt tails, for years, to come with me on a Mexico mission's trip, but like most pastors, he was fully involved with his local church ministry. Finally, he agreed to take me up on the offer and, there we were, crossing the US/Mexico border together. I love to take people in for their initial cross cultural experience because I remember how much I was impacted when our YWAM team drove into "the Juarez dump" for the first time.

I made sure that Stew was next to me in the passenger seat of our van. Before going to the Bible College, where we normally set up camp, I usually take the team for a little country tour. It does not take long before the landscape of "Mars" captures their attention and the silence in the van becomes rather distinct.

As we slowly maneuvered up a dirt road lined with mangy dogs sleeping under broken down cars, shacks for houses, open sewers, and yet friendly faces, I looked over at my friend Stew to find tears streaming down his face. I asked him how he was doing and he turned to me and said, "I get it...I get it..."

9). Teams should come as ambassadors of the King of Kings.

A church led short term mission team is not a service group coming to do volunteer work. We are ambassadors of the King of Kings and are representatives of His Kingdom. Real life ambassadors are diplomats. They are always sent on a mission for a specific place, time and assignment. They are trained to know about the nation they serve. When an ambassador speaks, he speaks for the nation he or she represents. Everything is paid for and taken care of by the sending nation. An ambassador never lacks anything. They have been given authority from their sending nation and cannot be arrested or deported.
They are not ambassadors in their own land but outside of their nation or country. Perhaps a better name for missionary is ambassador. As missionaries, long or short term, we are ambassadors or diplomats for our King, but most of us do not realize the special role we have.

Like the apostle Paul, we have the honor and privilege to be carriers of the name of Jesus. Acts 9:15: *But the Lord said to him, "Go, for he is a chosen vessel of Mine **to bear My name** before Gentiles, kings, and the children of Israel.* There is something powerful in a name. The following names will bring about a reaction in your heart as your read them: Obama, Ford, McDonalds, Elvis, Michael Jackson, Apple iPhone, Toyota, Lady Gaga, Hitler, Paul McCartney, Lady Di, Mother Theresa, Billy Graham, John Lennon, Islam, Nike, Walt Disney, Santa Claus, Microsoft, Moses, John Kennedy, and Martin Luther. With all of these names there is a name that is above every name. One day every knee will bow before the mighty name of Jesus. John Lennon will bow the knee; Lady Gaga will bow the knee. We have a high calling and assignment to represent Jesus to the world.

Being an ambassador is a kingly function. An ambassador is a representative of a nation and is appointed by a king. They are read by all men. They have this air about them, people are watching them and whether they like it or not they are witnesses – good or bad. A witness is someone who was there when it happened. When I was born again I was a witness at the scene. When people asked me how I knew that I was born again I would simply explain that I was there when it happened.

As ambassadors we have a ministry of the Spirit which is a ministry of reconciliation. These following verses in 2 Corinthians 5:18-20 should be a mission team memory verse. *"And all things are of God, who has reconciled us to Himself through Jesus Christ, and has given to us the ministry of reconciliation; whereas God was in Christ reconciling the world to Himself, not imputing their trespasses to them, and putting the word of reconciliation in us. Then we are ambassadors on behalf of Christ, as God exhorting through us, we beseech you on behalf of Christ, be reconciled to God."*

Every member of a short term mission team needs to understand that they are being sent out and empowered as ambassadors. They have been given authority in the name Jesus, the King of Kings. He has given them the keys to the Kingdom to open prison doors to set captives free and to stop the forces of darkness from getting in the way. He has equipped them with supernatural gifts such as discerning of spirits, words of knowledge and healings, so that they can perform their kingly functions as ambassadors as they reach out beyond the four walls of their churches.

10). Teams need to pray…pray…pray

Mission teams need to realize that they come with an assignment from the ultimate Head Office and have been given authority to act from the King Himself and have been endued with power from on high to be about their King's business. Not only that, The King goes with them into battle. He joins them on the mission by means of the Holy Spirit. For this reason prayer is vital. It is our means of communication with our ultimate team leader.

With the mission to go after Osama Bin Laden, I found it fascinating to watch the report on CNN and see how the president of the United States and his top leaders were fully included in the assignment. They were in direct communication with the mission team. In the same way, our leader, the King of Kings, wants to be in direct communication with us before, during and after every assignment that He sends us on.

The most successful and impactful teams that I have been part of have been where team members have prayed much beforehand, during the outreach and for the people they have reached out to. Groups need to have the perspective that it is God who will make a long term impact upon people's lives. No matter how good their drama may be, if the Holy Spirit is not breathing life into the presentation the outcome may be no more than a good show.

Statistics show that more people are healed when we pray for them than when they are not prayed for: *Selah*! I believe that every time we pray for someone something happens. We may not see the direct results, but God is at work during our prayer times. The people we pray for may not necessarily feel anything at the moment but it is important to assure them that as they come to God, He is a very generous and loving. God is for them and is out for their very best and desires to change them into His likeness.

Remember as your team prays for people, Jesus is the healer. One of the names of God is Jehovah Rapha. This literally means, I am healing; this is part of who I am. It is important to encourage people that Jesus is in our midst, the One whose very nature is Healing.

I also like to remind team members that language is no obstacle for God. He is as fluent in English and Spanish as He is in Mandarin.

In the Bible it is recorded that Jesus spent more time healing and setting people free than preaching.
I figure if Jesus needed healing to go along with the preaching of the gospel and His early disciples needed it, we certainly do, not only for our mission trips but for everyday living.

The Kingdom of God is the place where God rules, where darkness is dispelled. 1 John 3:8 says "*For this purpose the Son of God was manifested, that He might destroy the works of the devil."* The Kingdom of God is where light comes in, where health and healing rule and not sickness and disease. Jesus came to show and tell, what the Kingdom of God was truly like and He demonstrated the superior power of God's Kingdom over all of satan's opposition. Do we not need to see that today? Does not the world need to see the full gospel of Jesus Christ? Do we not need to bring this on our next mission trip? Would not the power of God make long term impacts on our short term mission trips?

Is it possible that even though the Lord has not changed, the church has? I believe the world is looking for disciples again who will take the healing out as Jesus did – out beyond the four walls of church buildings and do what Jesus did. He healed people in cities and villages, synagogues and homes, in the mountains and by the lake, by the sea and the roadside. What does that mean for us? Wherever you are, be open for business: The Father's business.

When teams, for example, visit families door to door they need to fully welcome the Holy Spirit to take a central role in their effort to share the gospel and to pray for the needs. Truly as it says in John 16:8 *"And when He (*Holy Spirit*) has come, He will convict the world of sin, and of righteousness and of judgment."*

I know that when we honor and recognize and value the presence of the Holy Spirit with us, through our prayers, He is more than willing to work in the lives of people we are reaching out to. I go with the attitude that every time I pray for someone, something happens. It is important to pray before we go out, while we go and after we come back.

Whether we like it or not, we are in a spiritual battle. When we are leaving for a mission trip we go with a purpose to overcome the kingdom of darkness and the enemy does not like this. Teams need to be aware that they have a foe who not only opposes what they are doing but he hates any attempt they make to set people free from the enemy's captivity. He does not have a problem with us meeting at church. He actually prefers this. But when he hears of our mission trip to Central America he begins to interfere and disrupt. Every member of the team needs to recognize that he or she has entered into a battle and, because of this, they need to put their armor on and dress like a soldier in God's army as is highlighted in Ephesians 6:11-18. Prayer is not the preparation for the battle, it is the battle.

My favorite place on earth

I had a favorite place on earth in Costa Rica. It was a large rock that I sat on in a fairly secluded place along the right shoreline of Playas del Coco. It was not easy to get there because I had to make my way along a very rocky section, which is why I went there. Most people preferred to stroll along the sand and so I did not get many visitors, except for the odd adventurer. Every time that I perched myself upon my rock and gazed upon the beauty of God's creation, I felt this wonderful presence of peace as if the Lord was saying, "Thanks for coming."

I cannot think of anything that was more important for my life as a missionary than my time spent sitting in my favorite place on earth. It was there where I dealt with my failures and shared openly and honestly about my apprehensions, questions and fears. I learned that I did not have to try to impress God with my prayers. I did pray and I did worship but mostly I just sat with Him. During these precious moments together, He helped me to stay connected and aligned to the simplicity of being a follower of Jesus.

I can attest to the reality that any long term impact that Debbie and I made on the mission field went back to our personal quiet times and prayer times as a couple.

11). Teams should come well prepared.

To make a long term impact, team leaders need to do their homework before going on a mission trip.

Following up on the last principal, it is important to find out from the Lord, first, where you are supposed to go. This decision needs to be in harmony with the mission direction of your local church or organization. As an arrow in the Lord's quiver, He wants to pull back the bow string, aim and release you to hit the target that He has in mind for you and your group. I believe this starts with a country. When the Lord called Debbie and me to Costa Rica I could not understand why He would not send us to Mexico. We had developed many contacts there over the years of leading mission teams to Tijuana and the Baja. We could have settled for what was familiar and easily accessible but that would have resulted in going on our mission trip and not His.

Where is the target that He wants your local church or organization to focus on and invest in?

I believe that the Lord has a specific strategy for every local church that fits into His overall strategy.

Before sending a team for the first time to Nicaragua, for example, I highly suggest that the team leader and pastor of the church go to scout out the land. I strongly believe that if a church is going to develop a strategy for missions, the pastor needs to be fully onboard to help spearhead the outreach. Further on he may not be actively going with the teams but has been to the country, has seen the needs and has met some of the leaders who his church members will be working with.

Before Debbie and I sold our house and bought our one way tickets to Costa Rica we came for a two week scouting trip to get a better assurance that this call to Central America was truly from the Lord. We met with the national leaders and heard their hearts about the general area of Costa Rica that they felt was the neediest and where they sensed was the best place to send us. After seven years of living in the western province of Guanacaste, we have certainly seen the wisdom of their recommendation and the Lord's direction every step of the way.

Once a country to reach out to has been established, team leaders should learn some of the basics about the culture, history and general rules of the nation they are going to serve. This can affect simple things like crossing the road. In Costa Rica the cars have the right of way and so pedestrians have to be extremely alert when they are close to traffic. In my home nation of Canada the pedestrians have the right of way and so the drivers have to be extra cautious when there are people close to the road. I have seen many North American tourists get upset when drivers do not even slow down when they step out on to the road. Their perception is that the Costa Rican drivers are rude for not stopping but the reality is that the Canadians did not do their homework before arriving here and unknowingly put themselves at risk when trying to do something simple as crossing the street.

This can also apply to elementary things as asking to pass the salt. In some cultures when sharing a meal with your guests, if you would like to use the salt shaker, the proper etiquette is to ask someone to please pass the salt. In another culture this would demonstrate poor manners because you are disturbing someone while they are eating. In this culture, the corrcct thing to do would be to reach across the table and take the salt shaker.

In the Cambodian culture it is outstandingly disrespectful to touch the top of someone's head. In our Canadian culture laying hands on someone's head while praying for them would be considered normal practice. Touching someone's head in the Cambodian context would be like Canadians praying for people by laying hands on their backsides. Imagine if we reversed the scenario, so that for the Cambodian Christians it was the norm to lay hands on someone's rear end to pray for them. How would your church members in Canada respond when a short term mission team from Cambodia starts praying for them by laying hands on their *derrieres*? Somebody did not do their homework.

These cultural differences and perspectives apply to many areas of life and so this type of information should be part of the training taught to the team before going. If you are looking at going to Honduras, for example, a great help for your team would be to invite a person from your community who has grown up in Honduras, to come and spend an evening with you. This way you can ask them all kinds of questions about their country and culture. Do you ask for someone to pass the salt or just reach over and take it? Is it ok to lays hands on someone's head? When greeting someone for the first time do I shake hands or is a hug appropriate? What about a kiss on the cheek? What should I wear to a church service? When visiting people door to door is it ok to wear shorts? Do people from Honduras like spicy food? What are some of the main differences that you have encountered while living in Canada?

Another part of the preparation time should be learning and practicing some of the rudimentary language expressions used in the country. If you are reaching out to a Latin American nation, team members should be able to know how to greet people in Spanish and be familiar with common expressions like "God bless you, thank you, please, see you later, where is the bathroom, the food is delicious" etc. I have discovered that people from another nation really appreciate every effort we make to speak their language.

Preparations should also include how the team is going to get their message out. If it is through the creative arts such as mime, drama or dance, make sure the team has spent quality rehearsal time during the months before the trip. Everything we do is a teaching to the people we are reaching out to. If we come with a well prepared and quality presentation this will be a motivation for others to value and to pursue excellence in their ministry.

Testimonies can provide opportunities for everyone on the team to be involved but, for them to be effective, they also need to be well presented. A three to five minute clear and focused testimony can be a powerful encouragement to others. In my experience they are most impactful when shared from the heart or from a brief outline rather than read from a paper. Part of the team ministry preparation should include times to practice testimonies, especially if an interpreter has to be used. Again, how a team ministers and shares is just as much a teaching as what they share and can provide opportunity for long term impact upon people's lives.

12). Teams need to export principles and a way of doing church that can be reproduced in the country they are visiting.

To make a long term impact a mission team needs to realize that what works in Vancouver, Canada may not transfer over to a rural church in Central America. It is important to export the gospel but not necessarily the whole form of the way we do church in North America. Teams need to think about what type of footprints they are leaving in the country they are setting foot in.

In her book, *We Are Not the Hero,* Jean Johnson captures this well. "When I use resources and methods local believers cannot easily reproduce, I create a roadblock for them. I make them feel powerless because they cannot do ministry "like Jean." As a result, local believers will often give up or find a missionary to do the work. This return to the missionary starts a chain of psychological and financial dependency on missionaries and churches abroad. I cannot even begin to emphasize how beneficial it is when I allow the organic context and the local people to supply the resources instead. Using restraint for the sake of reproducibility does not come naturally. There will be times when withholding seems callous." [6]

Jean goes on to say, "I am convinced that if missionaries were to only follow one missiological principle— the principle of reproducibility—

they would avoid most of the problems that strangle indigenous churches and keep them from mobilizing themselves to fulfill the Great Commission in their own context and beyond. If we use resources that are not available in the local context or are too expensive for the average local person to access, we have sabotaged reproducibility. If we dig a well for people, but do not empower them with the ability to maintain the well or capability to dig other wells, we have ignored reproducibility. The effectiveness of modeling is directly proportional to its reproducibility."[7]

The principle of ownership is also important to address. The first example involves a church building erected in a rural part of Ecuador by well-meaning North Americans. On one occasion a group of short-termers saw the well-built building and asked about it. Local people said, "We refer to this as the gringo church. Gringos came from North America and built it, but we do not use it. We have our own places of worship." Another example shares how a missionary told how he had taken a group of young people from North America to Guyana to build a church building. After three weeks of dedicated effort, the building was at last completed and presented to the local people. The North Americans returned home convinced that they had made a good contribution to needy people. Two years later the missionary, now back in the USA, got a letter from the people in Guyana. It read, "The roof on your church building is leaking. Please come and fix it." The importance of this is well understood by those who are familiar with issues of "ownership." [8]

This simple bamboo church in a rural community in Guanacaste, Costa Rica is a great example. I was very impressed to see how the local members of this church had taken the initiative to construct their own building including chairs, tables and benches.

It is very functional, fits in with the culture, works well in the climate and is very reproducible. With limited resources they were able to construct a church building for under $1,000.00? They can gather inside and feel a sense of accomplishment that this was a family project. They can think to themselves, "With the help of the Lord, we put this together." They had ownership.

I would much rather see this than a North American team coming in to build a North American style building with a North American style budget for the people in this rural community. What I would prefer to see is a North American team coming in to help these Costa Rican church members nail on the bamboo slats and screw on the tin roofing partnering with them to construct their own building: Costa Rican style.

This statement from a camel herder in Northern Kenya sums it up well, "When you can put your church on the back of my camel then I will think Christianity is meant for us Somalis." [9]

Chapter 5

<u>Missions in harmony with discipleship</u>

"God does not have a mission for His church in the world...
God has a church for His mission in the world."
Christopher Wright

 I really like my iPhone. I use it to tune my guitar, read my Bible, read books, and translate languages. I communicate to others via SKYPE, Facebook, and even use it as a phone. It is my alarm clock, flashlight, calendar, calculator, and camera plus it has a myriad of other uses. It is simple, so that anyone can use it, but highly effective.

Like my iPhone, this chapter is about a return to simplicity: a simple and yet highly effective method by which anyone can be involved in the process of making disciples who, in turn, make disciples.

The basis of missions is the call of the great commission: Go and make disciples. If you make this the foundation for your short term mission trip, you will see long term results. I believe that the "Go ye and make disciples" are the two main components that Jesus called us to pursue. I see them as two wheels on a bicycle. To move the bicycle ahead both wheels need to be working in harmony.

Often times mission teams come to do the "Go ye" part and present the gospel during church services, open air meetings or visiting families door to door, and measure the success of the mission trip by the number of salvations. They may see people make decisions to follow Jesus but if there is no model for follow up, many of the new converts will unfortunately fall by the wayside. Evangelism without the potential of discipleship in a local church is incomplete.

When Jesus said, "make disciples" the disciples understood it to mean more than simply getting someone to believe in Jesus. They interpreted it to mean that they should make out of others what Jesus made out of them. Robert Coleman explains the Great Commission in the following way: *"The Great Commission is not merely to go the to the ends of the earth preaching the gospel, nor to baptize a lot of converts into the name of the triune God, nor to teach them the precepts of Christ, but to 'make disciples'—to build people like themselves who were so constrained by the commission of Christ that they not only followed, but also led others to follow his way."*

The Great Commission compels Christians to focus on keeping people through discipleship as much as they focus on reaching people through evangelism. With the rise of the modern evangelical movement in North America in the 20th century came an over-emphasis on evangelism at the expense of discipleship. At the First International Consultation on Discipleship, John R.W. Stott called attention to the "strange and disturbing paradox" of the contemporary Christian situation. He warned,

"We have experienced enormous statistical growth without corresponding growth in discipleship. God is not pleased with superficial discipleship." [10] Bill Hull also addresses this issue by saying, *"The Great Commission has been worshiped but not obeyed. The church has tried to get world evangelization without disciple making."* [11]

The church must once again make discipleship a priority for a new generation of believers and this includes our mission programs. If not, we may be communicating that it is possible to come to Jesus for salvation without having any intention of being His disciples.

I have discovered, in my thirty one years of being involved with missions that simply handing out tracts or distributing Bibles or sharing the gospel door to door is the easy part and has not produced the amount of lasting fruit or long term impact that I would have hoped for.

Hundreds of raised hands for salvation and huge quantities of tracts and Bibles given out may look good on a mission's report but, in reality, may not be a good indicator of a fruitful mission's trip. I came to realize that I had done lots of seed sowing but very little cultivating.

It is like a farmer who sows seed but fails to cultivate and look after what he has sown. A good farmer needs to make sure that his plants have good soil prepared, an adequate amount of sunlight, water and fertilizer. He needs to protect his plants from harmful insects and weeds.

Robert E. Coleman, in his classic book <u>The Master Plan of Evangelism</u>, motivates us to use multiplication criteria to measure our effectiveness: *Are those who have followed us to Christ now leading others to him and teaching them to make disciples like ourselves? Note, it is not enough to rescue the perishing, though this is imperative; nor is it sufficient to build up newborn babes in the faith of Christ, although this too is necessary if the first fruit is to endure; in fact, it is not sufficient just to get them out winning souls, as commendable as this work may be. What really counts in the ultimate perpetuation of our work is the faithfulness with which our converts go out and make leaders out of their converts, not simply more followers... The test of any work of evangelism thus is not what is seen at the moment, or in the conference report, but in the effectiveness with which the work continues in the next generation. Similarly the criteria on which a church should measure its success is not how many new names are added to the roll nor how much the budget is increased, but rather how many Christians are actively winning souls and training them to win the multitudes.*

Evangelism and discipleship need to be intentional. We need to embrace the *missio* or the understanding that we are being sent for a purpose. The new phrase "missional" is being used often in Christian circles these days to promote the vision that we are called to be people on a mission: not our mission, but His mission.

Missional or opportunistic

I have discovered that there are two ways in which we can approach evangelism: missional or opportunistic. When I first arrived in Playas del Coco, as a full time missionary, I thought to myself, "Now what do we do?" The only thing that I could think of was go to the plaza downtown and hang out with the locals. I figured that I would make myself available to share the gospel with people who came my way: the opportunistic approach. I sat for quite a long time waiting for someone to come by until the Lord asked me, "I thought you were a missionary?" "I thought I was too." I replied. What He shared next opened my eyes to how He wanted me to approach people. "John, in this plaza there are people who are open, semi-open and some who are closed. Let me show you those who are open and then you go to them and start a conversation: the missional approach. Remember I am with you." I was receiving mission training 101 from the Lord Himself.

Every day I was able to share about Jesus to people who were open and receptive. I was amazed how easy this was even with my limited grasp on the language. Even more encouraging was the number of people who wanted to become followers of Jesus. The only drawback was that I had very little means by which to follow up and continue the discipleship process with them: a key missing ingredient. The Lord was about to show me that evangelism without discipleship is very ineffective. In the same way, discipleship without evangelism causes a church to stagnate.

The players of a basketball team, for example, need time to learn the rules and to practice their skills: dribbling the ball, shooting baskets and game strategy. If they never get to play the game, they become like a church group who spend all kinds of time hearing about God and learning methods on evangelism but never getting an opportunity to share the gospel. On the other hand if the basketball team spends all their time in game play and very little time in practicing the basics of the sport, they will be very ineffective in their matches. Similarly, a church that is only focused on evangelism will not produce mature and healthy disciples. We need evangelism and discipleship working together in harmony.

Since those early days in the park I have learned that if we are not intentional about going out to share the good news, this powerful message remains confined within the four walls of our church buildings or homes. Not matter how opportunistic we are the people are seldom going to come to us asking if they can hear the good news. A good farmer needs to take the seed to the soil rather than waiting for the soil to come to the seed. The reality is that we need to be both relational and relentless in both of these areas. For evangelism to be effective we need to be relational and intentional. For discipleship to be effective, we also need to be relational and intentional.

We also need to understand that the average person, for several reasons, is not inclined to come to our church services, even if we go to their house to invite them. They have their pre conceived ideas about church. They do not know anyone. Some think that they need to clean up their act before going. In my experience, some people will come to our events if they know we have things to give out: food, clothing, eye glasses, medical supplies etc. but the vast majority of people invited do not show up for our evangelistic church meetings, and so we end up trying to evangelize all of the Christians who normally do show up.

Rather than inviting people to our church meetings, I began to ask if they would be open to us coming back to visit them. I was surprised by the number of people who said that they had no intention of going to a church meeting but would be open to another visit or a meeting in their own home.

With this in mind I started to ponder the question, "What would happen if rather than asking the people to come to us, we started to ask the people if we, the church, could come to them?"

Since then I have been working on a method where evangelism works in harmony with discipleship. Before we can make disciples we need to look for them and find them. One of the best places to find them is in their homes.

Friendship Homes

I am developing a simple method of combining evangelism with discipleship that I have named "Hogares de Amistad" or in English, "Friendship Homes."

The concept is so simple that I do not know how we have missed it. Perhaps it is because we have this human tendency of taking the path of least resistance. Investing time in others requires sacrifice. Sacrifice is the price that will be required of us if we purpose to serve others.

The purpose of "Friendship Homes" is to look for families or individuals who do not have a relationship with the Lord and are not connected to a church family. Rather than asking them to come to our church events or meetings, we will be asking them if we can come back to visit them in the safety of their own homes or perhaps at a neighborhood coffee shop.

A mission team can make a long term impact if they can introduce this concept to the host church or churches in the country that they will be reaching out to and then helping them to begin to implement the process during their short term mission trip. Before the actual trip the mission team leader can communicate with the host church or churches the vision for "Friendship Homes" and then if the pastors are interested, the mission team can teach this concept to the church members and then partner with them to put it into practice over the following days of their trip.

A mission team can work with the host churches to visit people door to door but the responsibility for follow-up and discipleship will be more on the local church. This way the mission team and the local church can partner together to see long term impact. The church members will be prepared to continue this "Friendship Home" discipleship program over the months following the outreach.

After working on a simple format on how we could do this, I decided to try it out on one of our mission trips to Nicaragua in July of 2013. I led a team of pastors and leaders from our Foursquare Churches in Costa Rica.

After sharing the vision with members from three of the local churches who we were partnering with in Tipitapa, Nicaragua and then training them how to share the gospel and the basic vision of "Hogares de Amistad," we formed teams and went out into the neighborhoods around the churches.

After two hours of home visitations that afternoon and two hours the next morning our teams were able to lead 18 people to the Lord and helped another thirteen others get back into a relationship with the Lord.

Normally these results would be great indicators of a successful outreach, but for me the most exciting thing was that with these salvations we had eight new families to go back to and visit. Our hope is that after a time of relationship building these Nicaraguan church members can next invite their new friends to a church home group and then introduce them to the broader church family at a special event or Sunday morning service.

I led another team of leaders from Costa Rica to Nicaragua in August 2015. Over the week our group of 22 were involved in various activities: seminars for pastors, ministry to women and children, church services and practical work projects. The most impactful, for me, was our time of partnering together with a new church plant in a community called Marañonal, a suburb of Managua. The congregation was delighted that we had come to help them to share the gospel in their neighborhood. I shared that our hope was to find a few families that were not connected to the Lord nor attending any church. We formed several teams and proceeded to visit homes in the area. I led a group that consisted of two Costa Rica members and one person from the local church called "La Cosecha," the harvest. Over a two hour time period we visited the homes of several lovely families. When arriving at the home of Scarlet I felt something special about her as she warmly welcomed us. Although living in very humble conditions she pulled together some buckets and stools and invited us to sit down under a mango tree in her yard. Through our conversation we discovered that she was not part of a local church family but was very receptive as we shared the gospel with her. She showed a sincere desire to learn what it meant to be a follower of Jesus. When I asked her if she would like us to return to her home the next day, to continue our conversation, she was very agreeable.

The following morning our team brought some cookies and juice to share with Scarlet and her family. When we arrived her husband, Olman, also came to sit with us. He was very open as I shared my testimony with him. Along with Scarlet the day before, that morning he also decided to become a follower of Jesus. Later that day, we were able to bring the pastor over, as well, to meet the couple. That evening our team ministered at La Cosecha, the church that we were working with. I was very blessed to be able to welcome and introduce Scarlet and her family to the congregation. In the picture below is Scarlet, myself, Olman and Pastora Vicky.

Obviously there is a limited amount of ministry that a Short Term mission team can do within a one week time frame. For me, the greatest impact of this week of missions in Nicaragua was being able to introduce a family to the Lord and seeing them connected to a local church. Our short term neighborhood outreach was done in a way that the local church could continue the process of making disciples. This is a great way for Short Term missions to make a Long Term impact.

There are two problems with this method of evangelism combined with discipleship. It is not fast nor is it easy. Simply sowing the seed is easy. Giving out tracts and Bibles is easy. Sharing the gospel is easy. Giving out food and clothing is easy and it can make us feel good, but Jesus called us to more than this. He calls us to make disciples. This is not easy. This requires making an effort to spend time with people.

With this model of going to the people, these churches members now had a lot of work to do. It forced them to invest their time and energy in a few people. Maybe this is similar to what Jesus did with his disciples.

I think that when churches begin to use this simple model to combine evangelism with discipleship that we will begin to see, over time, an exponential growth of disciples in the church.

In the appendix I have included a simple format that can be used as a guide for leaders to help them with the discipleship process, as well as, methods and tools on how to share the gospel while visiting people in their homes.

Chapter 6

<u>Why Short Term Missions?</u>

"I believe that in each generation God has called enough men and women to evangelize all the yet unreached tribes of the earth. It is not God who does not call. It is man who will not respond!"
Isobel Kuhn, missionary to China and Thailand

Answering some of the criticisms

Over the years, I have been asked questions that address the validity of sending short term mission teams: Rather than sending teams, would it not be better to simply send money? Are not the benefits more for the people who are going than for those who are receiving teams? Are we not in danger of creating dependency with our giving or causing unintended harm by our kindness? Are we really making an impact? Is there really a need for full time missionaries anymore?

Money and Missions.

Clearly there is a cost to send a team of ten people to Costa Rica or where ever. As good stewards of the Lord's resources we need to ask ourselves, "Is this a good investment? Should we invest in short term missions?"

Unfortunately when I look at statistics and general studies done on church giving, in my estimation, we need to invest more in missions and not less. I have included a few examples.

For 15 years, the mission research and advocacy organization Empty Tomb, of Champaign, Ill., has analyzed the contributions and spending patterns of American churches. The latest report, "The State of Church Giving through 2003" [12] crunches the numbers for 41 Protestant denominations and surveys giving trends going back almost a century. In doing so, the study gives a not-too-flattering snapshot of the priorities of American Christians today.

"Churches on the whole are continuing to spend more on current members and less on the larger mission of the church and cutting back on missionaries," said Sylvia Ronsvalle. She is the Empty Tomb's executive vice president and the report's co-author.

The report shows that in 1920, the percentage of giving to missions from the total offering was 10.09 percent, just over a dime out of every dollar. In 2003, conservative and evangelical denominations gave 2.6 percent (about three cents per dollar). The combined average for overseas work is about two pennies per dollar.

A 2004 survey of 34 denominations showed that the average amount of total denominational budgets going to overseas missions was 2 percent. [13]

Another study by Ronsvalle showed that 85 percent of all church activity and funds is directed toward the internal operations of the congregation, such as staff salaries, utility expenses, and Sunday school materials. [14]

"Various studies conducted by George Barna during 2002 ... revealed that the average church in America gives only 5% of its income to missions, spending 95% on itself.

Almost 50 percent of the average church's budget goes to staff and personnel salaries. Missions and evangelism accounts for about 5 percent.
[15]

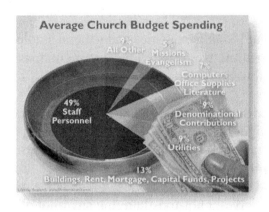

With these statistics in mind, to me, it does not look like we are over spending on missions.

"All the money needed to send and support an army of self-sacrificing, joy-spreading ambassadors is already in the church." — John Piper

It is estimated that Christians worldwide spend twice as much per year going to the more than 500 conferences to talk about missions then the total spent on doing missions. For this reason I encourage churches to send their members so that they can begin to learn what it means to be involved with missions rather than just hearing about it and talking about it. As I mentioned before, for me, missions was something I had to experience. I had to step out and do it, but there was a cost to this.

When Debbie and I received our acceptance letter to attend the YWAM discipleship training school in Edmonton, Alberta we were excited. Our only hindrance was the $5,000.00 tuition fee, taking six months off work and providing for our two children.

Two years previous to this, we had answered the call of the Lord, by leaving family and friends in Victoria to resettle in Campbell River. After giving up my well-paying job as a cement truck driver, and leaving my homeland, it took me almost a year to find a job. We were just starting to get ahead when the acceptance letter arrived.

I am sure our intentions looked irrational and perhaps irresponsible to the outside world, but we knew on the inside that God was calling us to go.

As Debbie and I sought the Lord for provision, we felt impressed to sell some of our furniture and our car. Often times the Lord will start His provision by using something that we have. Before feeding the 5,000 Jesus asked His disciples, Matthew 15:34 *"How many loaves of bread do you have? They said, seven, and a few fish."* From those few loaves and fish, Jesus was able to feed the multitudes. From the little that Debbie and I gave up, the Lord was able to multiply. A family from our Foursquare Church in Willow Point gave us a car. By September we had enough to pay for our tuition and were on our way to Edmonton.

Our three months of training and communal living were life changing. Our son, Karl, was on a home school program while our daughter, Karin, toddled around as a cute four year old. We were preparing for missions as a family.

After paying our $5,000.00, we had $100.00 left for spending money for the next six months. Although the tuition fee covered our meals and accommodations, we still needed money to purchase toiletries, gas for our car, plus the odd snack along the way. As the time for our outreach approached we had $6.00 left.

Debbie and I had been wrestling for weeks over the decision to continue on with the outreach to Mexico or not. What was going to be the determining factor: our lack of money or God's call? It was not until we had decided to go, even though we had no money, that God showed Himself strong.

The knock on the door came at 10:30 in the evening. Debbie and I were sitting rather forlorn in bed. It was the night before our team was scheduled to leave for Mexico, and we still had no money for the journey. As I opened the door, one our YWAM leaders handed me an envelope and apologized that she had forgotten to give it to us earlier that day. I am sure God had something to do with that. We thought for sure the letter was from a member our Foursquare Church back home, but the return address was from Victoria. Inside was a very nice note of encouragement plus a cheque for $100.00, from a couple we hardly knew.

There was no small stir in our little apartment that evening. We bounced on the bed like two little kids on Christmas morning.

Every mission's trip that I have been involved with has provided opportunities for God to show that He is, indeed, our provider. I often hear, "I would love to go on a short term mission's trip, but I cannot afford it." After my own experiences, I am more confident to share that the determining factor for going is not finances but faith. The question is not, "Can I afford this, but; is God calling me to this?" I have not seen Him fail yet. The truth is, "God does not fail."

"Rather than paying for the airfare, food and accommodations for ten church members to come to Costa Rica for two weeks, would it not be better to simply send you the money that we would have charged the team so that you can invest it into the needs down here?" This is another question that has been posed to me by church leaders who have come down to partner with us. From strictly a financial perspective, we could definitely benefit from the money spent on team transportation and accommodation, but we would lose, the team would lose, and the people receiving the team would lose. We would have extra money but no missionaries.

As much as our society wants to believe it, money is not going to solve the problems of this world. Money cannot be a substitute for a loving hug from a Canadian church member to a young fatherless boy in Mexico. It will never replace the encouragement received from a heartfelt testimony from a former drug dealer delivered from the bondage of a lifestyle of addiction. Money will never develop companionship between team members from Canada and Costa Rica. Money cannot preach the good news to the poor. It cannot lay hands on the sick and see them recover nor set the captives free. Money cannot teach a leadership seminar or put on a VBS for children in an impoverished neighborhood in Nicaragua. Money will never replace the fellowship from home that is so appreciated by full time missionaries on the field. I have found that a successful short term trip can revive and energize us and help us in our work through the teams evangelistic and service efforts. Money will never fulfill the great commission; people will.

I have often wondered, "Why has God provided so much financial blessing to some, while others live in poverty?" In reality, God tells us exactly what we should do with the abundance that we have been given: 2 Corinthians 9:10-11 *"He who supplies seed to the sower and bread for food will supply and multiply your seed for sowing and increase the harvest of your righteousness. You will be enriched in every way **to be generous in every way**, which through us will produce thanksgiving to God."* (Emphasis mine)

You will be enriched in every way so that you will be generous in every way. How we look at this is important. Prosperity theology would finish it like this: ". . . so that we might live in wealth, showing the world how much God blesses those who love him." But that is not how Paul finishes it. He says, "You will be made rich in every way *so that you can be generous in every way.*"

God does not make us rich so we can indulge ourselves and spoil our children, or so we can insulate ourselves from needing God's provision. God gives us abundant material blessing so that we can give it away, and give it generously. Yet, as we give, we must do so with much wisdom. There is a pitfall that we have to watch out for.

One of the hardest things for me, as a missionary, is seeing what comes in the offering at our church in Filadelfia, Costa Rica and comparing that to the offerings that we received at the church we pastored in Canada. An average Sunday morning offering in Canada was about what our Filadelfia church collects in one year. You may be thinking, "Well, that does sound a little bit lopsided but the cost of living is way lower in Costa Rica." Bananas and other tropical fruit maybe cheaper but overall food costs are about the same. Gas is the same price, clothing is more expensive in Costa Rica and cars are double the price. The national minimum wage here is still about $2.50 an hour. Being aware of this difference in economics, I have felt torn by my desire to help out and the reality that bringing in outside funds to do so is not the answer and can hurt more than help. This is where the pitfall comes in.

75

My biggest battle has been to stop trying to fix the poor economic level of the church in Filadelfia, for example, by using outside resources. This following story helped me to change my perspectives.

Steve Saint developed a DVD series called Missions Dilemma: Is There A Better Way To Do Missions? Within this series, Steve interviewed Christian leaders from around the world. "If there is one piece of advice you could give to North Americans of how to do missions better in your part of the world, what would it be? Steve's first interview was with, Oscar Muriu, a leader and pastor in Kenya Africa, who responded in the following manner: "You have an amazing capacity to resolve problems. Now, it's a great thing about Americans: the ability to innovate and to resolve problems. The downside of that is that when you come to our context, you don't know how to live with our problems. You see our poverty. You see our need. You see the places we're hurting. And, you have a great compassion to come and solve us, but life can't be solved that way. Many times well-intentioned Americans will come into our context and they try to fix my life. You can't fix my life! What I need is a brother who comes and gives me a shoulder to cry on and gives me space to express my pain, but doesn't try to fix me. When Jesus comes into the world he does not try to fix all the poverty, all the sickness, all the need, the political situation. He allows that to be, but he speaks grace and he speaks salvation and redemption within that context because there is a greater hope than this life itself. Now, this tendency to fix it has become a real issue so that some of the reserve we feel as Africans or as two-third world people is so many have come to fix us that O' Lord, please don't bring another person to fix us. We have been fixed so many times we are a real mess now. Please allow us to be us. Allow us to find God and to find faith in the reality of our need." [16]

Steve Saint, also gives some practical advice from lessons learned from his time spent with the Huaorani tribe of Ecuador. "Missions is not to go in and create and control church for other people nor be the church for them. It is not our job to insure that it functions. It is simply and only to plant the church in every people group and nurture it until it is able to propagate, govern and support itself. When missions go beyond that, then they are imposing themselves in the area of responsibility that belongs to the indigenous people and then everything gets out of whack." [17]

In his book *Missions That Heal*, Joel Wickre makes a great point. "People who are treated as helpless come to hold a lesser view of themselves. People who believe they are "blessed to be a blessing" and not in need themselves come to a lesser view of the people they serve. These victim and savior complexes create co-dependency that perpetuates the problems of poverty and far outweighs any temporary relief such missions provide …Poor people understand that getting help requires appearing helpless, and rich people unwittingly advance the helplessness of those they serve by seeing them as objects of charity, not equals."

Here is another quote that touched my heart. "Don't assume that we are poor and have nothing to give. When you do that, you insult God and diminish our ability to participate." [18]

Starting with a focus on needs amounts to starting a relationship with low-income people by asking them, "What is wrong with you? How can I fix you?" Given the nature of most poverty, it is difficult to imagine more harmful questions to both low-income people and to ourselves! Starting with such questions initiates the very dynamic that we need to avoid, a dynamic that confirms the feelings that we are superior, that they are inferior, and that they need us to fix them… Pouring in outside resources is not sustainable and only exacerbates the feelings of helplessness and inferiority that limits low-income people from being better stewards of their God-given talents and resources. When the church or ministry stops the flow of resources, it can leave behind individuals and communities that are more disempowered than ever before. [19]

Our role is to lead people of other nations to believe that God has visions to give them and that he will provide all they need from within themselves and among their own people. Our goal should be to facilitate the dreams of others, rather than to unfold our own dreams in someone else's neighborhood.

I now view more clearly that every person within each segment of society is a contributor and has many gifts and talents. We need to approach missions with the premise that we are not meant to be external saviors, and we need to understand that there are local champions everywhere, needing a word of encouragement to mobilize their local skills and resources.

Here is an example of two different well projects in Central America. The first project resulted in temporary relief, and the second project led to long-term systemic development. Bob Lupton shares about how his church from North America dug a well for a community in a village in Honduras. The village cheered with exuberance when the well was completed and water was available. When the team from North America revisited the village one year later, they found that the well wasn't working and the people had returned to their old methods of hauling water. The team quickly repaired the pump and eventually returned home. I wish I could tell you that when the team visited for the third time the villagers were using the well, but that is not the case. The well project in Honduras is an example of temporary change with no sustainability plan in mind. Lupton tells about another well project in Nicaragua that led to long-term systemic change. In this case, a local micro lending organization hired a community developer from North America. The community developer did not make a plan for the villagers in regard to a well, but instead facilitated the members of the village to make a plan. The villagers invested some of their own money and provided all the labor. The community developer accessed a Nicaraguan engineer who trained the villagers in how to maintain the well, set fees, collect payments, and manage finances. Not only did the well provide that immediate village with water, but they were able to sell water to other villages. This well project in Nicaragua is an example of aiming for long-term systemic transformation. [20]

I am working through this right now with our church in Filadelfia. They are in the process of starting up a children's feeding program for a needy community close by called Bambu. I was approached by the pastor of a local English church, who had heard about our desire to start up this ministry in Bambu. They wanted to come in and help us with supplies and organize this feeding program. As I met with the pastor and a few of his leaders I thanked them for their willingness to help out but shared with them that it is very important for the local church to own this feeding program. If someone from the outside comes in to provide the supplies for this it will take away the incentive from the local church members to be involved. The result will be apathy and indifference. Heartfelt ownership of a church or ministry is like the heart that pumps our blood; it is necessary for life.

As I shared with our church in Filadelfia that they were the owners of this feeding program I could see a sense of excitement rise up in them. Within ten minutes they had organized volunteers to bring food supplies necessary to start this ministry. The following week they had a planning meeting to set up a schedule for the members of the congregation to take an active part in the cooking, cleaning and serving of the meals. If someone from the outside wants to make a donation, this will be welcomed but the church is by no means dependent upon outside resources to make this work.

We welcome help from churches that want to partner with us as long as it does not set up any form of dependency.

I have used the term partnership often in this book. What I mean by this is two groups working together: helping each other, learning from each other and respecting each other. Partnership is not about one partner giving funds to the other partner. We need to be careful that it does not turn into a dependent-ship rather than a partner-ship. A true partnership needs to have true interchange and be absent of paternalism, which is a policy or practice of treating or governing people in a fatherly manner, especially by providing for their needs without giving them rights or responsibilities. If any degree of dominance exists in the partnership, local initiative is taken away.

We are looking for true partners who will come to give and to receive, to teach and to learn, to serve and to be served.

Short term mission trips do make an impact upon the need to give towards missions. In a George Barna study, statistics show that people are more likely to give money to something they have been a part of and personally had a hand in, allowing short-term missions to produce increased financial support for long-term mission work. Each person who participates in a short-term trip can share their experiences with their personal networks and encourage others to be involved through praying, giving or going. Short-term missions can produce a snowball of support for any given long-term project.

After his first mission trip, John Christiansen, a member of the church we were leading, summed it up well.

"I needed to experience this. For the first time in my life I see how materialism has captured our culture and how miserable we are in it.

When I first saw the poverty I was blown away: speechless. It took all I had to keep the tears in. I also do not do well traveling in a packed van for hours at a time, feeling like a sardine, but it was the best thing for me. We became family. ***I did not really give to missions before this trip but that is going to change****. I received far more from this experience than the Mexican people I went to serve. They taught me a lot, first and foremost that material things are not the means to happiness. To me, Mexico was like going to Mars and every one of us needs to go. "*

Are not the benefits more for the people who are going than for those who are receiving teams?

Let me simply say that, yes, there are great benefits for the people going, as well as, the people who are receiving teams. This should not be seen as a deterrent in sending mission teams. Actually, there are benefits for the sending church and the community that is receiving teams. Even the Lord benefits from our short term mission initiatives. Let us look at some of the benefits.

Benefits to the team members going:

1. Cultural perspective: Since much of our Christianity is largely defined by our culture, it is hard for us to discern between culture and true Christianity. As missionaries, we must endeavor to discern what is gospel and what is merely our own culture.

Only when we encounter another culture do we recognize the existence of our own culture as distinct; prior to that, we simply assume that our way of life and our interpretative horizon are universal. Not until I am exposed to another culture do I recognize myself as a cultural being, that is, as someone who has a particular way of life; prior to that, I simply assume that my way of life is also everyone else's.[21]

Having the opportunity to minister outside of our country or even outside of our own neighborhoods helps us to discern the difference between the two. We have much to learn from other cultures. Mexicans, for example, have taught me a lot about hospitality. The term "Mi casa es su casa." (My house is your house) is a genuine, heartfelt expression in Mexican society.

Kelly Minter has written a great article that gets to the heart of how missions can make a long term impact upon every one of us.

Why loving the poor changes you.

I touched down in Manaus, Brazil—The Gateway to the Amazon—and within an hour I was on a wooden boat sailing down the largest river in the world, blue and glassy with reflections of wool clouds and a crisp sky. I was there with Justice and Mercy International, a ministry to the forgotten people of the Amazon. I could have never imagined at the time how the course of this river—boasting pink dolphins, anacondas and caimans— would so affect the course of my life. That week we ministered in various villages that sit along the river's banks and we slept the nights in hammocks. Caimans clicked and piranhas splashed and all manner of species called and cooed under the canopy of dark. Still, the Amazon's people would prove the most exotic catalyst for change in my life.

*Perhaps the first thing the ribeirinhos (river people) taught me is that **the poor and forgotten desire something different than what we think they do.** In Western culture we're prone to rely on our stuff, resources and thoughtful solutions as the great big answer to most everything. But a fourteen year-old boy named Alexio reminded me that the needs of the heart are far deeper than what we attempt to fix with our wealth and resources.*

During one of the worst recorded floods in Amazon history, the swift rise of the river was mere centimeters from his stilted hut. The second oldest of ten, whose father and oldest brother had left the family, Aleixo's countenance wore the frightful responsibility. I encouraged him in his faith and quickly moved onto offering the help that any fix-it American would: food bags, extra fuel, a construction worker to shore up his home.

Aleixo politely nodded as though I had missed the point of our conversation. "No one has ever seen me before," he said. "God sent you to see me." His profound response reminded me that our most earnest need is to know that we have not been forgotten, that we are seen by Creator God. It took a teenage boy to poignantly reveal what the Scriptures have asserted all along: Jesus is the fulfillment of our deepest yearnings, rich and poor alike.

Two years later I helped put on our First Annual Jungle Pastor's Conference where my father taught jungle pastors the Bible for three solid days and I interviewed them. Each one recounted stories of miraculous healings, astounding testimonies of being rescued from addictions and violence, and proclamations of God's faithfulness while planting churches so deep in the jungle that snakes and deadly animals had to be cleared for the safe building of a church meeting place.

One pastor shared about the time his canoe had run out of fuel in the middle of a lashing storm. He prayed for rescue and his tank unexplainably filled with fuel and off he fled to safety. Another testified of being rescued out of witchcraft as a teenager by a sixty-five year-old praying neighbor. Still another about the time his family had run out of food and a parishioner delivered a fish to his door. "It tasted like a filet mignon" this pastor exclaimed, "because I knew I was where God wanted me."

Both my father and I were stunned at the jungle pastors' relentless commitment to prayer and their belief that God is really the all-powerful, all-knowing, all-present Savior He claims to be. As my dad so uncomfortably put it, "We may know more theology, but the believers in the jungle know more Jesus."

*After several years of traveling to the Amazon and becoming more aware of the poor in my own community, I see the call to love those on the fringes of society with greater clarity: **When we serve the poor, we realize we are not enough.** When we enter into the lives of the spiritually, physically, relationally, emotionally impoverished, we find that our resources are not enough; even our tightly wrapped theologies prove insufficient.*

The complexities and harshness of poverty force us to either abandon our belief in God or press harder into the Savior, Jesus Christ, the astounding news of the gospel. The people of the Amazon have propelled me even further toward the latter. And for them I am ever grateful. [22]

2. Appreciation for what we have: Sometimes we do not appreciate what we have until it is taken away. Walking into a migrant worker's camp where there is no electricity, flush toilets or clean water, and the average family sleeps, together, on wooden pallets for a bed, has made me appreciate the comforts of my Canadian home. I can flick a switch on the wall for light, drink clean tap water, and sleep on my Sears posturpedic pillow top bed.

Short term trip participants relocated to a foreign culture have the opportunity to undergo disorientation and realize life "back home" is not as rough or difficult as they may have thought; and the world is much larger than their hometown. The starting line of understanding the vastness of the world may turn into the beginning of comprehending the depth of our God.

3. Relationships established amongst the team members: A coffee break during a Sunday morning church service may offer an opportunity for relationship building, but becomes minimal in comparison to the close knit ties that can be formed during a two week mission trip.

4. Opens their eyes to the mission field: My Short Term Mission experience was the spark that ignited me to pursue the call to missions.

5. It has been the catalyst for some to pursue longer term mission assignments. We have had two couples from our church in Canada, Bill and Christina Clark, and Joel and Sally Frostad, who became involved on a full time basis: Joel and Sally for over eleven years.

Seventy-five percent of people surveyed who have participated in short-term trips said they were "life-changing," according to October 2008 mission statistics collected by the Barna Group. Twenty-five percent said their short-term mission experience increased their awareness of other people's struggles; 16 percent said it helped them gain knowledge about poverty, justice or the world; 11 percent said it increased their level of compassion; 9 percent said it enhanced their faith; another 9 percent said it expanded their spiritual understanding and 5 percent said it escalated their financial generosity.

Go as a Pilgrim, Not a Hero
Tucker McPherson has written a great article that challenges our mind set for going on a Short Term mission trip. He shares that if we go with the attitude of being on a pilgrimage, we go with the express purpose of learning and receiving more than giving. Rather than going with the purpose of changing the world we go with the purpose of changing ourselves.

Celtic Christians used to talk about spots they called "thin places," areas where they felt closer to God. For them, these hillsides or coves were areas where the membrane between heaven and earth was stretched taut, where believers could almost feel the hand of God just on the other side. We read about such thin places in the Bible—where God came down to meet us. Jacob wrestled with an angel near the ford of Jabbok, Moses talked with God on Mount Sinai. It's strange that God often met His faithful in wild, unfamiliar places—mountains and valleys far from home. And perhaps that's still true today. Sure, we can find thin places as close as a corner church or a neighborhood park or even parked on your bed in your very own bedroom. You probably know a few. But when we travel outside our comfort zones—when we venture out to unfamiliar places to seek out God—we often meet Him in unexpected and extraordinarily powerful ways.

Almost two million Americans from 40,000 churches and other groups go on short-term missions (STM) trips each year, and many of those 2 million do such trips year after year. These journeys can be great catalysts for spiritual growth and renewal and conduits for fellowship. But sometimes, if you're not careful, they can morph into little more than a vacation that doesn't do you or the people you're trying to help much good.

What Are Short-Term Mission Trips?
These short-term trips really are contemporary versions of an ancient Christian practice called pilgrimage. (Perhaps we should call them STPs.) A pilgrim goes on a journey to meet God in a faraway place, hoping to return a different person from the one who left. In medieval times, Europe in particular was crisscrossed with pilgrimage routes, with the destination usually being a notable church or site of a saint's relics.

Pilgrims had no illusions that they were going to "change the world" by their pilgrimage, but they surely did hope that being exposed to the world, and to the stories of the faithful saints, would change them. They were much more than tourists who travel simply for the fun of it (though medieval pilgrimages were often, appropriately, convivial and joyful affairs). Pilgrims travel for transformation. And that's a very good thing.

Like medieval pilgrims, too, short-term teams travel together in community, where we actually depend on one another to make it through unfamiliar and challenging experiences. In a pervasive culture of

*individualism, that too is a very good thing. When and where else will
most of us embrace a shared life of prayer and work for a week or more,
sharing cooking and cleaning, tears and laughter, in such close quarters?
In a nonstop world of distraction and diversion, STMs force us to focus
and pay attention.*

The Thing We Do Best
*When you start to awaken to the huge investment in and uneven returns
from STMs, it's natural to ask whether it wouldn't be much better simply
to raise the same amount of money and send it to our partners overseas as
cold, hard cash. But leaders from other countries would much rather open
the doors to short-term missionaries than simply receive a check in the
mail. They see the real potential of STMs: not the chance to get a wall
painted, a latrine built, or even a VBS taught, but to develop lasting
relationships with other Christians.*

*In fact, so highly do most hosts value relationship, they simply cannot
imagine that we would spend all this money and expend all the effort that
goes into a STM for anything other than building a lasting, deep
friendship and partnership in the gospel.*

*That's an important thing to keep in mind when you head off on a short-
term missions trip. While your church or sending body wants you to build
a schoolhouse or paint a church or conduct a Bible school, the people
whom you're being sent to want ... you. They want to share their stories
with you, and you to share with them. They want to walk and talk with you
about the gospel, the thing that brought the both of you together in the
first place.*

*Sure, you have a task to perform—to create something tangible that has,
hopefully, lasting value. But when you go on a mission's trip with the right
attitude, you'll often find that the most lasting, most valuable thing you've
done is to come seeking out those thin places with sincerity and humility.
And to search for those thin places together.* [23]

Benefits to the local church:

1. A local church that consistently sends out Short Term Mission teams
gives opportunity for their members to reach out beyond the borders of
their own community.

2. Our mission trips include a three month preparation time plus the trip itself. This lends itself to the deepening of relationships among the team members that continue beyond the actual outreach into the life of the church.

3. The congregation becomes for more supportive of the local church's mission vision.

4. Those who have a short term evangelistic experience outside of their own culture are more likely to gain a burden and a vision to minister at home. I have observed that members from my congregation, who have been on a Short Term Mission trip, tend to be more actively involved in local outreach initiatives than those who have not experienced a mission's encounter.

Benefits to the local churches who receive teams:

1. The zeal and enthusiasm of a STM team can be an encouragement to the local church members. The vision for mission and outreach can be stirred up so that when a STM team leaves, the church will continue to reach out to their community and beyond.

It is my belief that the most powerful thing a short-term visitor can do is to boost the self-esteem of the local believers. If we go and do big things with our resources and expertise, we often cause the local believers to feel inadequate.[24]

2. Just as our own STM teams learn cultural perspectives, the churches receiving teams can also learn from their visitors.

3. Long standing relationships and partnerships can be established and developed. Over the years we developed a strong Mexico-Canada connection between our Coastland's Foursquare district and many local Tijuana congregations. A church from Beausejour, Manitoba has sent teams from Canada over a three year period and have developed close ties especially with members from our church in Filadelfia. They plan to make Costa Rica a focus for their missions program and are looking at sending future teams to partner with us.

4. Just as Jesus was not well received in His own home town, a foreign team coming in to minister seems to cause people to take notice and listen more carefully.

5. Local host churches can also receive sound discipleship teaching from STM leaders that will help the church to grow spiritually.

6. The evangelistic efforts of a STM team can add new members to the congregation.

7. There are many practical areas of help, such as building renovations that can benefit host churches.

Benefits to the local community involved:

1. People get saved, healed and delivered.

2. A new local church can be planted. This happened on our very first Tijuana outreach. Our team of ten ventured into a Colonia called Guycura, where we proceeded to hold an open air meeting on an empty lot. About one hundred people bowed the knee to Jesus that day in March of 1988. As our team joined hands in a circle together with the new converts, I felt impressed to pray that God would raise up a church on this very land that we were standing. Within one year a church building was erected on that property. The young congregation not only had a building but also a pastor who was appointed from the Foursquare Bible Institute in Tijuana. That church continues to thrive today, 25 years later.

3. People hear the preaching of the Gospel of Jesus Christ.

Benefits to the Lord Himself:

1. We bring joy to the Lord of the harvest as He sees His children obeying the call to go and make disciples.

2. We bring relief to the heartache of God as people are transferred from the kingdom of darkness into the kingdom of Heaven.

3. We bless the heart of God as He sees nations in unity, partnering together in missions.

Are we not in danger of creating dependency with our giving or causing unintended harm by our kindness?

The answer to the question is, yes, we are in danger of creating dependency or creating unintended harm by our kindness. This should not be a deterrent to us sending teams but it should cause us to be *Serving with Eyes Wide Open* which is the title of a book by David A. Livermore. In his book David helps Christians understand the changing face of Christianity and how that affects short term missions. He takes a broad look at what the twenty-first-century church is doing on the mission field, the assumptions people make about Christianity, and what it takes to adapt effectively to new cultural contexts.

The other book that I recommend on this subject is *When Helping Hurts* by Steve Corbett and Brian Fikkert. The authors address some of the faulty assumptions that Christians have about the causes of poverty, resulting in the use of strategies that do considerable harm to poor people and themselves. This is a good read for anyone who works with the poor or in missions. *When Helping Hurts* provides foundational concepts, general principles and relevant applications in learning how to work with the needy resulting in an effective and holistic approach. A situation is assessed for whether relief, rehabilitation, or development is the best response to a situation. Short term mission efforts are addressed and economic development strategies appropriate for North American and international contexts are presented, including microenterprise development.

Timothy Mitchell, sums it up well in his book *Western Missionaries in Africa: One Missionary's Encounter with Self Reliance Thinking.* He is a missionary who implements training and mobilization among the Xhosa tribe in Transkei, South Africa. Timothy and his wife share about their temporary relapse into organizing the missionary task in accordance with their foreign funds and oversight: "Fundamental changes took place in our life and ministry. We now found ourselves working hand-in-hand with a Xhosa pastor. However, in our enthusiasm, we slipped into the age-old mistakes Western missionaries have so often made in Africa. As a result, we began reaping the enormous frustrations and disappointments that this approach can bring. Much as we longed for the local African leadership to take full responsibility and ownership for the operation, it just never happened. We found ourselves increasingly responsible for all the financing of the program and all the headaches of managing and motivating the whole concern. Although we aimed at sending out missionaries, very little fruit resulted. And although we planned to hand over leadership of the training center into local hands, it never happened. Our students graduated, but invariably went back into secular work. Eventually the school closed down and joined the long list of Western models in Africa that never worked— models which were never indigenized and often stood out as an embarrassment to the people.

We came to see that local initiative can come only from local vision and ownership. This can ONLY happen with local funding. Westerners struggle with this process, because it is initially much slower. There are any number of Western Christians in the world only too eager to sponsor projects in Africa, thus hastening a parasite mentality …We determined not to look outside the local community for any ministry funding. This is now working with exciting results! We teamed up with a man with the same thinking as ourselves and have seen in the last three years a highly missions-minded local church being established which is fully self-funded with full support for the pastor and his family and an appreciable monthly allowance to me, the "missionary", although most of our family salary continues to come from our own people." [25]

The third book that I recommend is *We Are Not the Hero; A Missionary's Guide for Sharing Christ Not a Culture of Dependency,* by Jean Johnson. One of her opening statements speaks volumes. "Missionaries aren't immune to the lure of heroism. The Movie "City of Joy" had a huge impact on me. I was amazed at how Dr. Max Lowe (Patrick Swayze), originally from Texas, and his mentor, an Irish woman (Pauline Collins), heroically involved their lives with the slum dwellers and lepers of Calcutta. There is something about their fantasticness that makes one say, "I want to do that too!" But after serving as a missionary in my own City of Joy— war-torn Phnom Penh, Cambodia— I have come to believe that these places do not need more Western heroes. I led a class discussion at a university on the topic of global perspectives. The students and I had just completed reading an article about how an American mission's team in northern Mexico made assumptions based on their own cultural experience and operated out of those assumptions. This dialogue led to the question, "Why do American Christians have a propensity to enter other countries as experts instead of learners and as heroes instead of servants?" A student quickly retorted, "Because Americans think they own

Christianity!" The student's statement was quite profound, and much was packed in that short response. How would people act if they thought they owned Christianity? Perhaps as heroes. We are here to bring you God! We are here to use North American dollars to make you better! We will show you how to do church the right way! Here is what I think! This is how you alleviate poverty!"

After eight years of living in Central America, I have learned that I am not the hero. My greatest desire now is to cheer on our local church heroes to govern themselves, support themselves and reproduce themselves in the natural soil and climate of their country. I encourage them to say, "We have a responsibility for the neighbors around us. We will ask God to enable us to minister to our neighbors through the Holy Spirit. Our knees will be worn out in prayer for our surrounding community. Our sweat will be the evidence of our love in action. Missionaries, pray for us that God will make us a relevant voice to our community."

A church in Costa Rica should look and sound like the society of which it is a part.

Our role needs to change from being perceived as the white knight riding in to rescue, to that of being a player-coach seeking to mobilize local resources to meet local needs. [26]

To make a long term impact we need to approach relief work with wisdom and care, but not stop reaching out. It is not the amount of missionaries that we send that will produce healthy churches. It is the quality of the missionaries and the soundness of their practice which will determine the outcome.

Is there really a need for full time missionaries anymore?

I had no intention of becoming a missionary. I was actually voted least likely to become a Christian in University. Well educated in the theory of evolution and a confessed atheist, my philosophy in life was, "Eat, drink and be merry for tomorrow you die." I sang along with Mick Jagger from the Rolling Stones, "I can't get no satisfaction!" And I tried…and I tried…

I became a missionary because missionaries first came to me. My journey from being a magician to missionary is unconventional. I didn't go to church; I didn't read the Bible. I didn't hang out with Christians. I was totally against God, but even in my rebellion, God - the ultimate missionary - came looking for me. You can read the full story about my incredible transformation in my book *Come Follow Go.*[27]

God did not sit in heaven, flip a switch, and send us hope. He did not do it by celestial remote control. He personally brought hope to us. He had human skin, breathed air, and walked our earth. Jesus was sent to us. John 3:17: *For God did not **send** His Son into the world to condemn the world, but that the world through Him might be saved.* Since our God is a missionary God, I am convinced that He is still in the sending business and that His people are a missionary people.

The final words of Jesus before He was taken up was a missionary call. Act 1:8: *But you shall receive power when the Holy Spirit has come upon you; and you shall be witnesses to Me in Jerusalem, and in all Judea and Samaria, and to the end of the earth."*

Jesus' original hearers understood that, in giving the Great Commission, Jesus was making a paradigm shift in regard to missions.
The Old Testament details a clear God-given mission to the Jewish people that they were to go out and bring people up to Jerusalem where they would worship with the one, True God. The mission was to bring people back to the Temple in Jerusalem. In the Great Commission, Jesus is changing the focus, explaining that now they need to simply go out and He would go with them there.

In the Old Testament when a stranger came into the Israel camp and wanted to find God, the people would point them to the Temple. It was pretty clear because there was a pillar of fire overhead. Jesus was well aware that there was a fire coming that would change everything.

Acts 2:1-5: *When the Day of Pentecost had fully come, they were all with one accord in one place.*
And suddenly there came a sound from heaven, as of a rushing mighty wind, and it filled the whole house where they were sitting. Then there appeared to them divided tongues, as of fire, and one sat upon each of them. And they were all filled with the Holy Spirit and began to speak with other tongues, as the Spirit gave them utterance. And there were dwelling in Jerusalem Jews, devout men, from every nation under heaven.

When the Holy Spirit fell upon the 120 disciples of Jesus gathered in the upper room it is clear that now the fire was upon each of the disciples who were now the temples of the Holy Spirit. The mission now had changed. Rather than trying to bring the people to the Temple, the temples were called to go out to where the people are. The missionary call was to start in Jerusalem and go out from there. Rather than bringing the nations **up** to Jerusalem, the people went out **from** Jerusalem to Judea, Samaria, and the ends of their earth.

The call to the ends of the earth is still valid today. As long as there is even one person who does not know God's love, we will still need missionaries.

A missionary is not someone who goes; it is someone who is sent on a mission. Luke 9:1-2: *Then He called His twelve disciples together and gave them power and authority over all demons, and to cure diseases. **He sent them** to preach the kingdom of God and to heal the sick.* The missionary is someone completing God's mission in his own church, then sent out to reproduce that church among other people.

When I look at the statistics acquired from the Joshua Project, the numbers cry out for God to send more missionaries.

In our world today we have about 16,804 people groups. Out of this there are 7,289 people groups who are still considered unreached. This works out to about 3 billion people who have not had anyone to share with them the gospel of Jesus Christ.

What is a people group? "For evangelization purposes, a people group is the largest group within which the Gospel can spread as a church planting movement without encountering barriers of understanding or acceptance"[28]

•865 million unreached Muslims or Islamic followers in 3330 cultural sub-groupings

•550 million unreached Hindus in 1660 cultural sub-groups

•150 million unreached Chinese in 830 groups

•275 million unreached Buddhists in 900 groups

•2550 unreached tribal groups (which are mainly animistic) with a total population of 140 million

•Forming a smaller -- though important -- unreached group are the 17 million Jews scattered across 134 countries

The 10/40 Window

You may have heard of the phrase the 10/40 window but unsure as to what it means. It is a way to refer to a group of countries and people who are in the least reached region of the world. These are countries stretching from northern Africa in the west through Asia to the east between 10 and 40 degrees north latitude. This band of countries is home to two thirds of the word's entire population – more than 4.4 billion people. By sheer volume of people and lack of religious freedom, this is a great area to focus our missionary efforts. Ninety percent of the people living in the 10/40 window are unevangelized. Many have never heard the Gospel message even once. If these groups are to be evangelized, we have to send Christians who will need to leave their own culture and enter another one where they will seek to share the gospel, and most likely having to learn a new language in order to communicate: namely missionaries. This kind of cross-cultural evangelism is required because there are people groups with no church movements that are understandable or relevant to them.

When we look at the five-fold ministries that are highlighted in the book of Ephesians, we see that their purpose is to equip the saints for the work of the ministry. Ephesians 4:11-12 *"And He Himself gave some to be apostles, some prophets, some evangelists, and some pastors and teachers, for the equipping of the saints for the work of ministry, for the edifying of the body of Christ."* The word apostle comes from two Greek words being put together. One means "from" and the other means "to send." The word missionary comes from the Latin *missio* meaning to "send." The linguistic equivalent of the Greek *apostolos* is "sent ones." I believe that it would be safe to infer that an integral role of a missionary would be to equip other missionaries for the work of the ministry.

I discovered that the people of Costa Rica seem to have favor with the Muslim world. Costa Rica does not have an army and so is not a threat plus their culture and skin color is similar to many of those living in the 10/40 window. On the other hand, a missionary from the United States, at this point in history, would not be received with the same favor. In God's wisdom and overall strategy for reaching the world, would it not make sense to send a missionary from Costa Rica to minister in Iran or other countries in the 10/40 window where they have more favor? With this in mind, I can see the value of sending Canadian or US missionaries to Costa Rica to help equip Costa Rican missionaries to minister in the 10/40 window.

I found that an important part of our ministry here in Costa Rica had to do with this equipping process. The eight churches that we have helped to plant have definitely been impacted by the call to take the gospel out beyond the four walls of the church buildings. Many of the pastors have been with me on short term mission trips to Nicaragua and all have received mission teams from the US and Canada.

I also helped to promote missions and equip missionaries within our province of Guanacaste, as well as, on the national level. Missions cannot be learned by simply reading a book like this or listening to a stirring missionary testimony. We learn as we go. For this reason, I led teams of Costa Rican pastors and leaders to Nicaragua, with the purpose that they, as well, would begin to send missionaries.

Jesus had a great method of teaching His disciples about missions. The whole concept of sending STM teams was actually modeled by Jesus. He begins their training by explaining to them what His mission or purpose was all about. Luke 4:43: *"I must preach the kingdom of God to the other cities also, because **for this purpose I have been sent**."* A little while later we read that the disciples were with Jesus watching Him do the "stuff." Luke 8:1: *Now it came to pass, afterward, that He went through every city and village, preaching and bringing the glad tidings of the kingdom of God. And the twelve were with him.* Then the next chapter, He says, ok gentlemen, now you do it. Luke 9:1: *Then He called His twelve disciples together and gave them power and authority over all demons and to cure diseases. He sent them to preach the kingdom.* In the following chapter He calls even more people on a short term mission's trip. Luke 10:1: *After these things the Lord appointed seventy others also, and sent them two by two before His face into every city and place where He Himself was about to go.* Sounds like missions to me.

As I led mission teams of Costa Rican pastors and leaders to Nicaragua, I realized that my purpose was to equip them to lead their own mission teams in the future. Following the model that Jesus showed us, on the first trip they were with me and watched how I did it. I challenged them to learn because the next time some of them would take a leadership role. The second time I came along for the trip and watched but asked one of the previous team members to take the lead. I was there to assist but not to be in charge. The next step is for them to lead a team on their own, while I wait to hear good reports on how the lame were made to walk and the captives were set free. My hope for the future is to see an army of Costa Rican and Nicaraguan missionaries venturing forth beyond Central America and into the 10/40 window.

I figured that while I was in Nicaragua, I might as well encourage and challenge some of them to send mission teams to Costa Rica. After helping to promote missions we are hoping to encourage them, as well, to continue beyond Nicaragua unto the ends of the earth.

Another area where missionaries are needed today is in Bible translation. Thankfully there are Bibles in many languages. However, it is estimated that there are around 2000 languages which still do not have any of God's Word available to them in printed form. There are many more than that which do not have a complete copy of the Bible. Many of these people groups do not have a missionary who can speak their language or have a Bible believer among their native language speakers.

Do not think that the golden age of Bible translations is in the past. It is true that the most commonly spoken languages have a Bible available to them now. But there are many languages yet to read about God's precious good news in their own tongue. The opportunity to have a greater personal influence in a translation project is right now.

I believe there is a perception out there that a "real missionary" needs to own a pith helmet and, with machete in hand, be searching for an unreached tribe somewhere deep in the Amazon jungle.

Not all missionaries are pioneer missionaries. For example, outside and within the 10/40 window there are many countries which are closed to missions. Traditional missionaries cannot go in and establish churches freely or even witness on a personal level in some cases. Some countries will allow personal witnessing, but limit public meetings and printed literature such as Bibles.

While a "closed country" may not allow traditional missionaries into their borders, some will legally allow them into the country through alternate work opportunities. There is therefore a need for missionaries to come in wearing a stethoscope or a nurse's uniform. Some have gone into countries as legitimate coffee buyers, technology engineers, doctors, school teachers and social workers. These are just some of the many ways that missionaries can get into limited access countries.

There are myriads of needs on the mission field today. The gospel must go to the 10/40 window so that the Muslim and Hindu worlds can be reached for Christ. However, I agree with Dr. Jack Arnold who writes, "The greatest need, in my opinion and the opinion of most missiologists who are on the cutting edge of world missions, is to train the pastors and Christian leaders in the Third World countries where the gospel is spreading like wildfire. There are millions of people coming to Christ in China, Asia, Africa, South America, and Eastern Europe. It is estimated that right now there is a need to train two million pastors to meet the needs of an exploding Church, and by the year 2015 that number will escalate to five million. How can we accomplish this monumental task?" [29]

Another reason for the need for missionaries today has to do with cross-pollination. If a region of the world—or the world church—is cut off, if no more "outsiders" arrive to share their experience of faith, walk their streets, teach in their schools, the people of that region will become more and more focused only on themselves and become ingrown. Selfishness will grow. Understanding and support for the church's mission around the world will decline. The same will happen to any part of the world that cuts itself off and no longer sends its sons and daughters to help others. We need more cross-cultural missionaries from all regions of the world church reaching out to one another. We need to be a church that goes from everywhere to everywhere.

As a missionary I realized that my call did not stop with winning people to Christ and establishing a church. That alone was not fulfilling the Great Commission. My ultimate goal was to establish a church and disciple the believers so that they can go and make more disciples and send out more missionaries. I believe that a natural result of making disciples will be people who hear to call to missions. In fact, I do not believe that the church has a missionary problem. It simply just needs to follow the mandate of Jesus to go and make more disciples. The result of making disciples will be more leaders and missionaries.

Missionaries do make a difference. In 1989 there were only four known Christians living in Mongolia. That country now has an estimated 10,000 indigenous believers. These results did not come without years of sacrifice and perseverance on part of the missionaries who were sent there to serve. It is interesting to note that the Mongolian church sends out more missionaries per capita than anywhere else in the world.[30]

Even if we were in a country that did not allow for us to plant a traditional church, God's plan has never changed and we must never lose sight of that. We are called to obey and to serve where He sends us. It may take several generations for a church to be established. The results will come but we may never live to see them except through eyes of faith. We must never lose sight of God's plan.

Obviously the 10/40 window has a great need for missionaries, but the Lord did not call my wife and me to that region of the world. Some people have questioned me whether Mexico or Costa Rica needs another missionary. It really does not matter whether you or I think that Costa Rica needs another missionary. It matters that I believe God has called me to Central America to do a work and I have to obey His will.

Is there still a need for missionaries today? The call for more missionaries is clear, but we need to make room for them. In every church there is a percentage of people, the explorers, who are always looking over the wall with this longing in their hearts to go beyond the borders of their church. I am one of those. If I were to choose to be a farmer or explorer there would be no hesitation for me to leave the farm. I would have been leading a wagon train heading west rather than settling in to cultivate my farm in Minnesota. I believe we need both, the cultivators and the explorers. My challenge to the church leaders who are reading this book is to begin to make opportunities for that thirty percent of your congregation who make up your explorers. I heartily agree with this quote by Harold Cook. "The life of a missionary program in a local church depends largely upon the leadership. Someone has to have the interest, the vision, the initiative to inaugurate a program, plus the persistence to carry it through. The pastor should be that leader."

If the leaders in the church do not have their focus on the mission, the people will not either. If there is silence on missions from the pulpit it will be difficult to stimulate mission's interest or missionary support in the pew. The explorers will seek other frontiers beyond the walls of the church to get involved with, perhaps the Rotary or the Lion's club.

"The mark of a great church is not its seating capacity, but its sending capacity." — Mike Stachura

There seems to be a perception in the church that the great commission to "go" is reserved for some elite, radical, extra special, secret service agents who are called to this kind of ministry. I believe the problem is that we have far too many secret service agents for Christ. We become so secret that nobody knows we are Christians.

The question that I would like to propose is, "What is so special about you that you cannot be used of God?"

I have heard lots of excuses over the years like, "Well… I just don't like talking to people. I'm not very good at talking before a crowd. I'm a little shy." I was an introvert, I used to major on shy and I was definitely a non-talker. I stuttered all through my school years. I am even limited in my ability to speak Spanish. I love to share with my Latino audiences, "How many here speak Spanish?" With smiles on their faces, they all raise their hands. I continue, "If God can use me, a shy, stuttering, introvert, who speaks Spanish at a grade one level, He can use anybody here to share the gospel. No one has any excuses, besides God loves to show Himself strong in our weakness."

Yea but

Along with the excuses, I also hear what I call the "Yea buts."

"Yea but… I'm not ready to 'go' to be a missionary in Bangladesh." I respond, "Ok, how about starting with your next door neighbor or that person you work with or who sits next to at your school?" You do not have to go far to be a missionary. It could be to the local *Trick and Joke shop.*

"Yea but… aren't there people here in Vancouver that need to hear the gospel?" I gently question, "Yes, there are… so what are you doing to reach them? By the way, out of 52 weeks in the year, I do not think it is overboard to use two of them for a short term mission's trip that goes beyond your community."

"Yea but…I'm not sure that I have a call to go." My reply, "So, if you have not heard the call to go then I presume you have heard a clear call to stay." (Selah)

"Yea but…I'm not the witnessing type." I say, "Yea but, you are. We are all witnesses. We are either good witness or bad witnesses; but we are witnesses."

"Yea but…I don't feel led." With this one I try not to respond, but I am thinking, "I just think it is a different kind of lead."

"Yea but… I need more training." I look back at my first opportunity to share the gospel. I did not know Romans Road or even the Four Spiritual Laws. All I knew was that something happened to me and whatever that was; my friend, Stew, needed it as well. I led someone to the Lord a week after I got saved. My first convert became a pastor in full time ministry for over 25 years. I am all for training, but when it comes to leading people to the Lord, how much training do you need?

I see a world that is experiencing increased birth pangs: major earthquakes, wars and rumors of wars. As we speak, great fear and hopelessness, recession, climate change, billions in the valley of decision, people empty and hungry and we have great news to share, the gift of eternal life. And we wonder about feeling led, and whether or not we should get involved with reaching out to people or whether we need more missionaries today?

This following vision for the lost received by William Booth brings a poignant summary to this question.

A vision for the Lost

By William Booth, Founder of the Salvation Army.

On a recent journey I found myself thinking about the multitudes around me. They were living carelessly in the most open and shameless rebellion against God, without a thought for their eternal welfare. As I looked out of the coach window, I seemed to see them all…millions of people given up to their drink, pleasure, dancing and their music, their business, anxieties, politics and troubles. Ignorant – wilfully ignorant in many cases – and in other instances knowing all about the truth and not caring at all. Suddenly, as I thought about them I had a vision.

In it I saw a dark and stormy ocean over which black clouds hung heavily. Every now and then vivid lightening flashed and loud thunder rolled, while the winds drove foaming waves into a tempest that was claiming lives. There were myriad's cursing, struggling and drowning, and as I watched some of them sank to rise no more.

The rock of safety

Then I noticed a mighty rock that rose up out of the dark angry ocean. Its summit towered high above the platform. Onto this platform, I saw with delight that a number of the poor struggling wretches were continually climbing out of the angry ocean. And I saw a few of those who were already safe on the platform helping others onto the rock. Many were working with ladders, ropes and boats to rescue those who were drowning. Occasionally someone actually jumped into the water, regardless of the consequences in their passion to "rescue the perishing".

I hardly know which sight delighted me more – the sight of the people rescued, or the devotion and self-sacrifice of those had who rescued them.

Looking more closely, I realized that the people on the platform were quite a mixed company. They occupied themselves in different ways. Some spent their days trading while others amused themselves by dressing up for the admiration of their peers. Many were chiefly concerned with eating and drinking and yet others were taken up with arguing about the people that had already been rescued. Only very few of them made it their business to rescue people from the sea.

What puzzled me most was the fact that although all of them had been rescued from the ocean at one time or other, nearly everyone seemed to have forgotten about it. And what seemed equally strange was that they did not even seem to care about the people who were drowning right before their eyes – many of whom were their own spouses, brothers and sisters and even their own children.

The Call

Those on the rock had received a call from the one who had Himself gone down into the sea. They'd heard His voice and felt that they ought to obey it – or at least so they said. They professed to love Him and to sympathize with Him in the task He had undertaken. But, they were so distracted by their professions, pleasures and their preparation for going to the mainland that they did not help Him. So the multitude went on right before them struggling, shrieking and drowning in the darkness.

And then I noticed that some of the people on the platform were crying out to Him to come to them! Many wanted Him to spend His time and strength in making them happier. Others wanted Him to take away various

101

doubts and misgivings they had concerning the truth of some letters He had written to them. Some wanted Him to make them feel more secure on the rock -so secure that they would be quite sure that they would never slip off again into the ocean.

So they would meet and climbing high on the rock they would cry, "Come to us! Come and help us!" And all the while He was down among those drowning in the sea trying to rescue them and looking to those on the rock for help.

The vision understood

And then I understood it all. The sea was the ocean of human existence. The lightening was the piercing truth coming from Jehovah's Throne. The thunder was the distant echoing of God's wrath. The multitudes struggling in the stormy sea were 'the Lost', ungodly people of every kindred, tongue and nation. That great sheltering rock represented Calvary, the place where Jesus had died for them. And the people on it were those who had been rescued. The way they used their energies, gifts and time represented the occupations and amusements of those who had been saved. The handful of determined ones that risked their lives to save the perishing were the true soldiers of the cross. The One calling on the rescued to help Him rescue others was Jesus Himself.

A time to act

Fellow Christians, you have been rescued from the waters, yet He is still in the sea calling for your help. Don't be deceived by appearances – men and things are not what they seem. All who are not on the rock are in the sea!

Jesus is in the midst of this dying multitude, struggling to save them. He wants you to jump in and help. Will you jump or will you linger on the bank, singing and praying about perishing souls? Lay aside your shame and pride, your cares about the opinions of others and all the selfish loves that have held you back for so long, and rush to the rescue of these dying men and women.

Unquestionably the surging sea is dark and dangerous. The leap means difficulty, scorn and suffering for everyone who takes it. Yet He who beckons you from the sea knows what it will mean – and knowing, He still bids to you to come.

You have enjoyed your Christianity long enough. Going down among the perishing crowds is your duty. From now on your ease will depend on sharing their pain and your heaven in going into the very jaws of hell to rescue them. Now what will you do?

Appendix

Leaders Guide for Friendship Homes

The following information can be used as a handout for those who want to teach this process to the host church that your team will be visiting. This is available in Spanish on our website www.missionteams.info

The purpose of Friendship Homes is to provide a means to disciple people who are interested in learning more about the ways of the Lord. Rather than asking them to come to our church events or meetings, we will be asking them if we can come back to visit them in the safety of their own homes or in a neutral place like a coffee shop or a park.

Rather than asking the people to come to us, the church, it is time for the church to ask if we can come to the people.

The process for this is very simple. During our time of visiting families in their homes, we ask if the person or family would like to learn more about the teachings of Jesus. All they need is a bible and a place to meet. We simply ask, "When would be a good time and where we be a good place for us to meet?" If they do not have a bible we will provide one for them.

The format for the meeting is also very simple. It is based upon building a friendship with new people and introducing them to Jesus. Friendship Homes is all about introducing people to the best friend they could ever have, Jesus Christ.

Start with some refreshments: coffee, juice, cookies etc. Fellowship should be the basis of each group. If possible, the church members should provide refreshments for the first few meetings.

After about 20 - 30 minutes of getting to know one another, the leader should thank everyone for coming and open in prayer.

The leader's role is to ensure that everyone has the opportunity to participate and that the group stays on course with the meeting format. A good rule of thumb is that no one should share twice before every person has had a chance to share once. In Friendship Home groups the leader is more of a facilitator than a teacher.

Five Easy Steps for the meeting

Step 1). Give each person a chance to share what they are thankful for.

Step 2). Ask people to share some things that may be causing stress in their life right now. What are some of the challenges they are facing?

Step 3). How can other members of the group help to meet some of these needs?

Step 4). Discovery Bible Study

This, as well, needs to be simple and reproducible so that anyone can learn to facilitate it.

Since we are followers of Jesus, a good starting point can be the teachings of Jesus: the beatitudes, His parables etc. For example, for one meeting the group can read the parable of the sower and the next week study what Jesus taught about prayer. With this in mind, the leader needs to come prepared with a scripture passage for the meeting. Since we are dealing with new Christians or even pre-Christians, I suggest that we start with smaller portions of scripture and build from there.

The beauty of this is that we have no extra papers, books or tapes that would need to be reproduced and handed out. Our discipleship manual is the Bible and our main instructor is the Holy Spirit who in reality is our personal trainer.

1. Read the passage of Scripture that has been selected by the leader, for example, the parable of the Good Samaritan. Members of the group can take turns in reading, if they wish.

3. What does this scripture mean? Members can share briefly using their own words what this scripture means to them. It is important to focus on

the passage, what it says, what it means, and what we hear God asking us to obey.

4. How will we respond to this passage? What am I going to obey? Start by saying, "I will do ... in response to the Scripture." Try to share things that can be measured so that the members of the group can be accountable to each other.

Step 5). Encourage the group members to begin to look for opportunities to share their experience with others: friends and neighbors etc.

This step is very important if we want to train disciples who make more disciples, not just members of the church.

Making disciples who make disciples

Often times, we are pleased if someone believes and joins the church, but the commandment that Jesus gave us is much more than that. He wants these new believers to become true disciples. And what do the disciples do? Every disciple must learn to obey the commands of Jesus, including witnessing to others and then training these new believers to repeat the process. Every disciple makes a disciple.

George Barna underscored some significant insights from this research on how people become Christians. "Just as our nation's culture has changed dramatically in the last 30 years, so has the way in which people come to Christ," he explained. "The weekend church service is no longer the primary mechanism for salvation decisions; only one out of every ten believers who makes a decision to follow Christ does so in a church setting or service. On the other hand, personal relationships have become even more important in evangelism, with a majority of salvation decisions coming in direct response to an invitation given by a family member or friend."

With this in mind, ask the members of the group to make a list of people who they can begin to pray for. We must put the work of the Holy Spirit central in the discipleship process. It is He who goes before us to convict people of their sins and to prepare their hearts to receive the good news that we hopefully will have opportunity to share with them. John 16:8 And when He has come, He will convict the world of sin, and of righteousness, and of judgment. This list can include friends, family members, neighbors, fellow workers or students at their college. It might be someone they meet on a regular basis at a bakery, coffee shop or the person who cleans their house.

Typically, the longer people have been believers, the less they will reach out to others because their circle of non-Christian friends has diminished or they are too busy with other ministerial responsibilities, and so it is important for new Christians to tap into their sphere of influence so that the gospel can continue to spread to new people. This is the key if we want to see a multiplication of disciples who make disciples.

A traditional Bible study, or cell group rarely comes with the purpose to reproduce other cell groups or train disciples to train disciples. For multiplication of disciples to happen there must come a time where the new believer is released to start his own "Friendship Home" group, at the same time continuing on with his original group. Since the new believer already has a network of people who they have some form of relationship with, the best time to reach their network is when the new believer still has connections with these people. This is where many church leaders might have a struggle because they are used to a pattern that follows the order of believe, mature and serve. As a new believer matures he or she will eventually be ready to serve. In the New Testament, believers matured through service; following the progression - Believe - Serve - Mature. In some Christian ministries, we evaluate the maturity of a believer on the basis of how much you know. But the New Testament assesses the maturity of a believer on the basis of how much they obey.

Too often, our current understanding of the word disciple or be discipled conveys the idea of receiving and not giving. Jesus taught his followers to share with others everything they received. Once the new believer is familiar with the format of the Friendship Home group he or she should be encouraged to look for opportunities to start their own group, rather than invite their friends or neighbors to their original group. We need to trust that every Christian has the Holy Spirit as their personal trainer always at their side. They also have their Friendship Home group leaders to refer to when difficult questions or situations arise. A new believer then would continue to receive training from their original Friendship Home group, as well as, put that training into practice by forming their own group.

Sharing the gospel from home to home

Here are some good guidelines for teams as they prepare to visit families home to home.
As we approach people in their homes, we need to do so with dignity, respect and much love. We do not have anything to sell but we do have good news to offer. We need to go with a smile on our face.

Remember that the joy of the Lord is our strength. We need to be real and not coming across as door to door salesmen. Each family that we encounter has a history and each person is unique. Some will be open and others closed. We are not called to force anything upon anybody and so it is important that we be kind, respectful and loving towards everyone we meet.

First impressions are very important and so we want to be as real and as natural as possible. Try not to sound like you are delivering a canned speech. Here is a sample conversation that might be helpful. "Good morning. How are you today? My name is Peter and with me are Paul and Mary. May I ask your name please? How long have you lived here? What a beautiful home you have… We are visiting from Canada and are here to support the local Church in this community. We are here to do a simple survey of this neighborhood. Do you have a few minutes available to answer a few questions?" The vast majority of people will be open to doing the survey. During this time you should be able to discern how to continue the conversation as you are led by the Holy Spirit. There is no formula here because every person and situation is different, but you do want to be sensitive to the Holy Spirit to see if the people are open to hearing the good news.

There are many good tools and methods available by which we can share the gospel. The two methods that I have found to be the most effective are the Evangecube and pocket testament Gospel of John. The Evangecube is simple, effective and captivates the attention of the people we are sharing with. It also comes with a tract that explains and illustrates what was shown. The Gospel of John also comes with a very good gospel presentation that goes along the same lines as the Evangecube. The cube is the key that opens the door to share the gospel, while the Gospel of John is the key that helps to open the door for discipleship.

How to order the Evangecube and the Pocket size Gospel of John

Evangecube: They can be purchased via the following website http://www.e3resources.org/ecube-go-6-pack/ These are less expensive by purchasing them in packs of 6.

The corresponding tracts are also available for purchase http://www.e3resources.org/etracts/
These are available in many languages including Spanish.

Gospel of John: The website to order supplies of these is http://ptl.org
These are also available in many languages.

For more information and practical ideas for your next mission trip please go to our website www.missionteams.info

Incarnational approach

There are basically two ways that we can connect with people. One is the incarnational approach. Be a follower of Jesus in your community. Be the best neighbor in your neighborhood. Simply follow the call of Jesus to love our neighbor. Be the best worker at your work place. Be someone who everyone likes to be around. Be like Jesus who was a friend of sinners. When we do this, people will naturally be drawn to us and opportunities will arise when they ask us for help, or prayer or they ask us about our faith. These are times where we need to be ready to share the good news and ask if they would like to learn more about the teachings of Jesus. This becomes a great opportunity to introduce them to "Friendship Homes" and ask the question "Where would you like to meet and what time is good for you?"

The other approach is to go on a mission. Be proactive. Just as Jesus sent His disciples on short term mission trips He still does that today. I believe it is important to organize short term mission trips into our communities and beyond. This helps to mobilize the members of the church and gives them opportunity to go and make disciples.

Let us first look at how Paul reached out to people.

1Corinthians 9:19 For though I am free from all men, I have made myself a servant to all, that I might win the more;
9:20 and to the Jews I became as a Jew, that I might win Jews; to those who are under the law, as under the law, that I might win those who are under the law;
9:21 to those who are without law, as without law (not being without law toward God, but under law toward Christ), that I might win those who are without law;
9:22 to the weak I became as weak, that I might win the weak. I have become all things to all men, that I might by all means save some.
9:23 Now this I do for the gospel's sake, that I may be partaker of it with you. (NKJV)

Paul treated everyone he met as individuals. He knew he had to approach a Jewish person, who was under the law, differently from a Greek who was not under the law. He treated someone who was not under the law in a way that this person could relate to him. He became like the other person so he could speak their language, so to speak, and communicate with them according to their way of thinking. He became all things to all men, but always with the "cause" in mind.

In our modern days, we can learn from this to be sensitive in how we approach people with the gospel and the way we do church. With this in mind, it is very important that we get to know the people whom we are trying to reach with the gospel.

Perhaps our first step should be to get to know the thoughts and perspectives of the people in our communities. What is their perception of the church? What are the needs of the community? How can we pray for them? How many do not attend church? What are they looking for in a church?

Community Survey

I have discovered that doing a survey will help connect members of the church to their neighborhood and demonstrates that we care for the community. Not only does it help us to know the thoughts of the people in the area but it is also a non-threatening way to approach people who we may not know. This is also a very effective way to include members of your mission team as they visit families door to door. They can practice how to say the questions in Spanish well before the trip. With the help of the Holy Spirit we should be able to discern where the family is at spiritually and whether or not we have an open door to share the gospel. Most people are very open to a time of prayer. Here is an example of a survey that can be used.

1. ¿Qué crees que es la mayor necesidad en esta comunidad?
What do you think is the major need in this community?

2. ¿Está usted asistiendo activamente a alguna iglesia?
Are you actively involved in a Church?

3. ¿Por qué cree usted que la mayoría de las personas no asisten a la iglesia?
What do you think is the main reason why people do not attend Church?

4. Si usted fuera a buscar una iglesia para asistir, ¿qué tipo de cosas le busca?
If you were to look for a Church to attend, what type of things would you be looking for?

5. ¿Qué consejo le puede dar a una nueva iglesia que realmente quiere ser útil para las personas en la comunidad? (O bien, ¿Qué podemos hacer por usted?)
What advice would you give to a new church that really wants to help the people in the community?

6. Nos gustaría orar por usted y su familia. ¿Hay alguna necesidad de oración que le gustaría incluir en nuestra lista?
With your permission, we would like to pray for you and your family. Do you have any needs that you would like to include in our list?

Nombre: (Name)

Dirección: (Address)

Celular: (Cell phone)

Other book by John Overholt

Come Follow Go: *Getting back to the simple mission of following Jesus.*
Venid Seguidme Id: *(Spanish version) La simple misión de seguir a Jesús.*

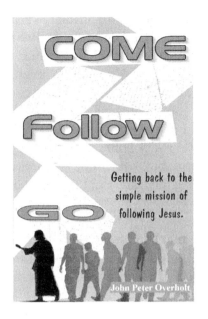 

What would your church look like, if Jesus was invited to be the pastor of it? How would church growth be affected if every member whole heartedly invited Jesus to be the Lord of their lives? How would discipleship training and evangelism in your church be transformed if every member invited the Holy Spirit to be their full time personal trainer? Is this not what we are called to? Why have we drifted so far from the simple mission of following Jesus?

This book is about a return to simplicity: a simple and yet highly effective church where everyone is involved as followers of Jesus and doing what He is calling them to do: a missional church. The church is us, but it is not just for us.

As the lead pastor of a church for sixteen years, John Overholt discovered that more spiritual activity and programs do not necessarily lead to more church growth. He worked hard to keep up with the newest trends in Christianity. He found himself paddling his church down one trending stream after another: Dr. Del Tackett (The Truth Project), John & Paula

Sandford (Elijah House training), C. Peter Wagner (New Apostolic Reformation). He set up a local church Bible Institute (Lifeline) and provided training in Hermeneutics, Apologetics, Christian counselling, New and Old Testament survey etc. The church members had to complete assignments, write exams and were handed diplomas for passing the courses. Along with this they had times of focusing on Spiritual Warfare, teaching on the Gifts of the Spirit and then the Baptism of the Holy Spirit. They had seminars on discovering your ministry gifts, finances, and healing. He promoted retreats and seminars for couples, men, women, and youth. They received training in every evangelistic method that he could find: Evangelism Explosion, the Alpha Course, being a Contagious Christian, teachings on the Four Spiritual Laws, Romans Road, Salvation bracelets and distributing the Jesus video to every home in the city. These programs and methods are valid and helpful, but; something was missing. He saw himself as a busy farmer cultivating the same field over and over again.

John remembers his feelings of discontentment and frustration after taking his church through a Cleansing Stream program for the third time thinking after it was finished, "Now what do we do?" He had run out of programs. The programs that we had gone through, in themselves, were good and he was sure helped many members of his congregation, but again he thought to himself, "How much cleansing stream does one person need? It was then that he received a very clear and penetrating question from the Lord. "John, if I was the pastor of your church what would I teach your congregation and what would I have you doing?" He thought to himself, "Well... if Jesus came to pastor this church...He would probably teach the same things He taught the early church and call them to do the same things He had called His early disciples to do...How simple is that?" As he started to ponder the ramifications of this, he could sense a lightness come into his spirit. It was like a veil was lifted from his eyes and he could see the simplicity and yet the great significance of inviting Jesus to come and shepherd the Campbell River Foursquare church.

As you read his story he continues to describe how an encounter with God took him from being a Magician and owner of a Trick and Joke shop into the mission field, first with YWAM (Youth With A Mission) and then with the Foursquare Church of Canada. This book has great insights and inspiration for anyone considering the call to world missions: the simple mission of following Jesus.

"Come Follow Go" has taken many years to write. We can teach a lot of things but we can only impart what we have lived. This book has been lived and has much to impart.

About the author

After emigrating from Norway, I started grade one with a very limited grasp of the English language, but with the help of a wonderful and caring teacher, I learned quickly. During this first year of school, I developed a stuttering problem that I still live with today. I dreaded any kind of class reading situation. I was frustrated many times during my school days when the teacher asked a question in class. I was a good student but never dared to raise my hand. Even worse were times when I was singled out and would play dumb, even though I knew the answer. I got to a place where I resigned myself to a life of silence rather than continually face the embarrassment of stumbling over the words I spoke.

I will never forget the day when my grade eleven teacher announced his next English assignment. Everyone in the class was required to do an oral report. As my stomach knotted up over the news, my inside displeasure, I am sure, became evident by the absolute look of dread on my face. The teacher was not even aware of my speech impediment, until I started into one of the most agonizing few minutes of my life. I had a three-minute talk that took me ten minutes and felt like an hour. I felt humiliated and dumb.

I find it fascinating that I now stand before a class (a church congregation) every Sunday morning to give a speech. Even more incredible is the fact that I am writing a book. Stunted in my communication skills, I disliked English and was not into writing at all in school. I remember laboring, for what seemed like hours, to compose a simple one-paragraph school assignment. The Lord truly likes to show Himself strong in our weaknesses.

Acknowledgments

To my precious wife, Debbie:
The journey has not always been easy but I appreciate how you have stood by me and walked with me to the ends of the earth and back.

To my children, Karl and Karin
In many ways the call of the Lord not only includes mom and dad, but involves the whole family. Being MK's, (missionary kids) has not been easy for you, especially not having your parents around at family events: birthdays, Christmas dinners, school plays etc. Facebook and SKYPE are great but they do not replace our personal times together. Thank you for understanding. We love you.

To my good friend, Stew Motteram:
Although now with the Lord, he had always been a great encourager to me.

To the wonderful leaders and people who we have met in Mexico, Costa Rica and Nicaragua:
Thanks for being so gracious and hospitable to our visiting Canadian teams. I know that you are sincere when you shake my hand, smile and say, "Mi casa es su casa."

End Notes

[1] Youth with a Mission was founded by Loren Cunningham and has become the forerunner of short term mission teams worldwide. For more information about YWAM check out their website www.ywam.com

[2] The Discipleship Training School is comprised of a three month, communal type living, classroom training course followed by a three month missions outreach.

[3] Deuteronomy 28:23.

[4] Come Follow Go: Getting back to the simple mission of following Jesus.

http://www.amazon.com/Come-Follow-Go-Getting-following-ebook/dp/B00A85S1JO/ref=sr_1_1?s=digital-text&ie=UTF8&qid=1385068895&sr=1-1&keywords=come+follow+go

[5] (variations of this also credited to G. K. Chesterson, Thomas Carlyle and Charles Haddon Spurgeon)

[6] Johnson, Jean (2012-10-16). We Are Not the Hero (Kindle Locations 1215). Deep River Books. Kindle Edition.

[7] Johnson, Jean (2012-10-16). We Are Not the Hero (Kindle Locations 1246). Deep River Books. Kindle Edition.

[8] How short term missions can go wrong. Two awesome problems. http://www.google.ca/url?sa=t&rct=j&q=&esrc=s&source=web&cd=15&ved=0CFIQFjAEOAo&url=http%3A%2F%2Fwww.ijfm.org%2FPDFs_IJFM%2F21_1_PDFs%2F27_34_Schwartz.pdf&ei=uBrJVJWyEYGBgwS9uIDgDw&usg=AFQjCNFChonYBZdmQTQGE6VtYOm9ppHR4Q&bvm=bv.84607526,d.eXY

[9] Malcolm Hunter, foreword to David Phillips, Peoples on the Move: Introducing the Nomads of the World (Pasadena, CA: William Carey Library, 2001), XIII.

[10] John R.W. Stott, "*Make Disciples, Not Just Converts*: Evangelism without Discipleship Dispenses Cheap Grace." Christianity Today, October 25, 1999 Vol. 43, No. 12, Page 28.

[11] Bill Hull, *"The Disciple Making Pastor."* Page 27.

[12] Statistics available at emptytomb.org

[13] John L. Ronsvalle and Sylvia Ronsvalle, The State of Church Giving through 2000 (Champaign, Ill.: Empty Tomb, 2002), 20.

[14] Ronsvalle, 13

[15] Lifeway Research, Average Church Budget Spending, n.d.

[16] Johnson, Jean (2012-10-16). *We Are Not the Hero* (Kindle Locations 150-156). Deep River Books. Kindle Edition.

[17] Quoted in Rick Wood, *"Fighting Dependency Among the 'Aucas'*: An Interview with Steve Saint by Rick Wood," Miss Assemblies of God World Missions, "Encouraging Church Planting," The Intercessor & World Report, June 7, 2011, Vol. 11, No. 25, 1.ion Frontiers, May– June 1998, 12. http:// www.adopt-a-people.org/ articles/ dependency.pdf

[18] Assemblies of God World Missions, *"Encouraging Church Planting,"* The Intercessor & World Report, June 7, 2011, Vol. 11, No. 25, 1.

[19] Steve Corbett and Brian Fikkert, When Helping Hurts: How to Alleviate Poverty Without Hurting the Poor And Yourself (Chicago, IL: Moody Publishers, 2009), 125–126.

[20] Bob Lupton, *"Vacationaries,"* The Mennonite, June 16, 2009.

[21] Jeanne Choy Tate, *"Studying the Bible across Cultures: Towards an Intercultural Hermeneutic."* Prepared specially for the CANAAC-CANACOM Joint Assembly/ Council meeting in Georgetown, Guyana, February 25– 29, 2008. http:// www.canaac.org/ wpcontent/ uploads/ 2009/ 04/ studying_the_bible_across_cultures.pdf

[22] http://www.christianitytoday.com/edstetzer/2014/august/why-loving-poor-changes-you-guest-post-by-kelly-minter.html

[23] Excerpt from Go, But Go Wisely: Finding Your Way as You Go on Mission (GMI Books, 2015). This book explores mission principles and trends to consider and includes articles from more than a dozen authors about different kinds of ministry you could pursue. http://www.gmi.org/products/books/gmibooks/go-go-wisely

[24] Johnson, Jean (2012-10-16). *We Are Not the Hero* (Kindle Locations 4589). Deep River Books. Kindle Edition.

[25] Timothy Mitchell, *"Western Missionaries in Africa: One Missionary's Encounter with Self-Reliance Thinking,"* World Mission Associates, 2009. http:// www.wmausa.org/ page.aspx? id = 83847

[26] Steve Corbett and Brian Fikkert, *When Helping Hurts: How to Alleviate Poverty Without Hurting the Poor And You* (http://www.joshuaproject.net/great-commission-statistics.php) (Chicago, IL: Moody Publishers, 2009), 125– 126.)

[27] http://www.amazon.ca/Come-Follow-Go-Getting-following-ebook/dp/B00A85S1JO

[28] Source: 1982 Lausanne Committee Chicago meeting.

[29] Dr. Jack Arnold, *Another Look at Missions for the New Millennium.*

[30] Reported by Brian Hogan, *We Are Not The Hero*, location 1100

Made in the USA
Columbia, SC
22 April 2018